SO-ADF-081

REVERSE LICENSING

REVERSE LICENSING

International Technology Transfer to the United States

Manuchehr Shahrokhi

PRAEGER

New York
Westport, Connecticut
London

230981

338.973
S 525

1 0001 000 020 657

Library of Congress Cataloging-in-Publication Data

Shahrokhi, Manuchehr.
  Reverse licensing.

  Bibliography: p.
  Includes index.
  1. License agreements—United States.
2. Technology transfer—Law and legislation—
United States. 3. Foreign licensing agreements.
I. Title.
KF3145.S47   1987   346.7304'8   86–25230
  ISBN 0-275-92258-8   (alk. paper)

Copyright © 1987 by Manuchehr Shahrokhi

All rights reserved. No portion of this book may be
reproduced, by any process or technique, without the
express written consent of the publisher.

Library of Congress Catalog Card Number: 86–25230
ISBN: 0-275-92258-8

First published in 1987.

Praeger Publishers, 521 Fifth Avenue, New York, NY 10175
A division of Greenwood Press, Inc.

Printed in the United States of America

The paper used in this book complies with the Permanent
Paper Standard issued by the National Information Standards
Organization (Z39.48–1984).

10 9 8 7 6 5 4 3 2 1

To My Family

Contents

Acknowledgments

This book would not have been possible without the contributions and assistance of many individuals. Thanks and appreciation are expressed to those who either provided me with excellent insights, comments, and support or reviewed parts of this book.

Special acknowledgments go to Dr. Lee C. Nehrt for his invaluable ideas, directions, and encouragement throughout the study. Also, Dr. Riad A. Ajami and Dr. Phillip M. Carroll provided me with invaluable editorial comments and insights during hours of discussion throughout the research period.

Dr. Joseph Penbera, Dr. Howard Whitney, Mr. Kenneth Kentosh, Dr. Godfrey Ibom of Franklin University, Mr. Gary James of James & Associates, and Mr. Rafael Underwood supported me in the research and gave me encouragement in one way or another. I am indebted to these gentlemen and am very grateful.

Dr. Mary E. Mogee and Mr. R. David Belli of the U.S. Department of Commerce; Mr. William Riley, Jr., of the Battelle Memorial Institute; Mr. David Urey of USX and the Licensing Executive Society; Mr. William Dolle of Lodge and Shipley, Inc.; Mr. Ben Dillon of Masstron, Inc.; Dr. Ehsan Nikbakht; Rassoul Yazdipour; C. W. Walker; and Dr. Farok Contractor went out of their way and devoted many hours of their precious time either to discussing international technology licensing issues with me or to providing me with excellent comments and data. Special thanks to all these people.

Finally, special thanks are due to Catherine Woods, my editor at Praeger, and to Mr. Kathy Hutton and Susan Litt, who edited, typed, and corrected hundreds of pages of this book before it finally was right. These people are to be commended for their excellent work under constant pressure.

Acronyms

COMECON	Council for Mutual Economic Assistance
FDI	foreign direct investment
FSA	firm-specific advantage
GDP	gross domestic product
GNP	gross national product
IPLC	international product life cycle
LCM	licensing cycle model
LDC	less-developed country
LES	Licensing Executive Society
MNC	multinational corporation
MNE	multinational enterprise
NASA	National Aeronautics and Space Administration
NIH	"not invented here" (syndrome)
NPV	net present value
PLC	product life cycle
R&D	research and development
SIC	standard industrial code
TLC	technology life cycle
UNCTAD	U.N. Conference on Trade and Development
UNIDO	U.N. Industrial Development Organization
WIPO	World Intellectual Property Organization

1

Introduction

STATEMENT OF THE PROBLEM

This book focuses on international transfer of technology into the United States. The U.S. licensees, as the recipients of technology, their characteristics and motivations, and the types of licensed technology and license agreements are germane to this research study. Licensing as an international marketing (sourcing) strategy is the means for such transfers. This study evaluates the viability of taking a license as an alternative growth strategy from the U.S. licensees' standpoint: reverse licensing.[1]

Reverse licensing will be evaluated as a bridge or a transfer mechanism between two groups of firms. The first group consists of thousands of U.S. manufacturing firms that need new technology for their survival. The new technology will provide them with an extension on their product life cycle (PLC). Small and medium-sized U.S. manufacturing firms are of special interest in this study.

The second group consists of thousands of small and medium-sized foreign firms. This group has the technology but lacks the resources to exploit the U.S. market directly. The scarce resources for this group are financial, marketing, and production, among others. Reverse licensing could provide its firms with the required international transfer mechanism.

Small and medium-sized firms are of special interest in this study because of their importance in the economy of each state and of the nation. Their importance in the U.S. economy is shown in a 1984 presidential report:[2]

- There are 14.3 million nonfarm businesses in the United States. Approximately 99.7 percent of these businesses are small by U.S. Small Business Administration standards [no more than 99 employees].

- From 1980 through 1982 large firms lost 1.7 million net jobs; most of these losses were concentrated in manufacturing (-1.5 million), retail trade (-0.2 million), wholesale trade (-0.3 million), and transportation (-0.1 million).

- Between 1980 and 1982, small businesses generated 2.65 million new jobs, more than offsetting the 1.7 million lost by large businesses. Small business has led the way in job creation during the recovery.

- Small business employs 48 percent of the private nonfarm work force, accounts for 42 percent of sales, and generates approximately 38 percent of the U.S. gross national product (GNP).

- Firms with fewer than 100 employees generated 51 percent of the net new jobs increase from 1976 to 1980. During the 1980–82 recession, small business enterprises with fewer than 20 employees generated all the net new jobs in the economy.

The above statistics show the importance of small firms in the U.S. economy. Yet, the statistics for business failures and bankruptcies clearly reveal which firms suffer most in an economic downturn and recession:

- Ninety percent of approximately 400,000 business that dissolve each year do so voluntarily—for instance, because of the retirement of the owner.

- Ninety-nine percent of the failed business have fewer than 100 employees; over 80 percent are less than 10 years old.[3]

Table 1.1 shows the changes in the number of business failures and bankruptcies during both economic recession and expansion. During the 1981–82 recession and the 1982–83 recovery, the percentage changes in business failures and bankruptcies are of special concern.

The number of business failures and bankruptcies may be a confusing indicator of real success and failure. It is

TABLE 1.1 Business Failures and Bankruptcies, 1980-June 1984

	Failures	Change (annual rate)	Bankruptcies	Change (annual rate)
Jan.-June 1984	15,235	0.6	33,167	-0.2
Jan.-June 1983	15,137	--	33,225	--
1983	31,334	23.6	58,898	-10.5
1982	25,346	48.7	65,807	38.4
1981	17,044	45.4	47,555	9.6
1980	11,719	--	43,374	--

Source: The State of Small Business: A Report of the President Transmitted to the Congress (Washington, D.C.: Small Business Administration/U.S. Government Printing Office, 1985), p. 13.

normal for areas with high economic growth to have high failure rates during economic expansion. Also, regions with slower growth are expected to have high bankruptcy rates.

. . . Nationally, business bankruptcies declined 2 percent between January and June 1983, compared with the same months in 1982. Then bankruptcy decline has been more dramatic in areas affected by the 1981–82 recession: 21 percent in the Middle Atlantic states, 12 percent in the New England region, and 2 percent in the East North Central industrial states, as these regions experienced significant recovery during 1983.

Recent increases in the bankruptcies and failures, however, in the West South Central, Mountain and Pacific regions have shown that the failure/bankruptcy index is a confusing indicator. Areas with significant economic growth like the Mountain states (Montana, Idaho, Wyoming, Colorado, New Mexico, Arizona, Utah, Nevada) usually have high business failures and high bankruptcies because of their continuing rapid business formation. Regions with slower growth, however, can also have high failure rates because of a poor business climate in the area (e.g., the Midwest industrial states during the 1981–1982 recession).[4]

Many small U.S. firms are forced into bankruptcy because they have one or few products. Once their existing product(s) reach the declining stage of the PLC, they have to close their doors.

Most of these small and medium-sized firms are unaware of foreign sources of technology. Those which know of overseas sources find no established mechanism or clearing house to tap those sources. In most cases, this is not true of large multinational corporations (MNCs).

Large U.S. MNCs have been utilizing this international marketing (sourcing) strategy since the mid-1960s. They have tapped the foreign sources and have taken licenses from foreign licensors whose technology fits their existing product lines or marketing channels. They have not limited themselves to U.S. allies, utilizing technology from the Soviet Union and other Eastern bloc countries.[5]

For instance, as of 1984, in the state of Ohio alone, approximately 120 manufacturing firms had acquired licenses from foreign firms. (A complete profile on these Ohio licensees is in Chapter 6 of this book.) The research hypotheses (see Chapter 5) have been empirically tested, using these Ohio licensees as the research sample.

On the other hand, to most U.S. MNCs, licensing is a residual international marketing strategy, particularly when they want to expand or to penetrate foreign markets.[6] In Chapter 2, evidence will be provided for such ignorance on the part of U.S. firms.

To show the importance of manufacturing firms in the U.S. economy, as of 1982, almost 32 percent of U.S. enterprises were in manufacturing industries. With structural changes in the U.S. economy and stiff international competition, this sector of the economy has been among the hardest hit in the recent economic downturns. In the state of Ohio, traditionally an industrial state, the manufacturing sector is still responsible for more than one-third of the employment. Table 1.2 shows the distribution of employment by firm size.

States react differently to economic slowdowns and economic recoveries:

New business incorporations increased 6.6 percent in the United States from January to June 1983, compared with the same period in 1982. The Midwest industrial states (Ohio, Michigan, Illinois, Indiana, and Wisconsin) were adversely affected by the 1981–1982 recession and had a larger increase in incorporations in the first half of 1983 (7 percent) than the rest of the United States. High unemploy-

TABLE 1.2 Percent Change in Employment by Firm Size, Selected Periods

		Number of Employees					
	Total	1-19	20-99	100	100-499	500	500+
Total employment, 1976	75,961,361						
Percent of total employment in each size class, 1976	100.00	20.5	16.9	37.4	14.3	51.7	48.3

	Job Growth (number)	Job Growth as Percent of Total Employment	Job Growth Attributable to Each Size Class					
			1-19	20-99	100	100-499	500	500+
1976-82	11,870,978	15.6	38.5	14.1	52.6	9.8	62.4	37.6
1976-80	10,891,982	14.3	29.1	13.4	42.5	10.6	53.1	46.9
1976-78	6,426,986	8.5	36.3	15.8	52.1	10.4	62.5	37.5
1978-80	4,464,996	5.4	29.9	5.9	35.8	7.3	43.1	56.9
1980-82	978,997	1.1	232.6	-9.8	222.8	-31.4	191.4	-91.4
1982-84	6,302,000	7.3	--	--	--	--	--	--

Source: The State of Small Business: A Report of the President Transmitted to the Congress (Washington, D.C.: Small Business Administration/U.S. Government Printing Office, 1985), p. 22.

ment during the 1981–1982 period may have helped stimulate this new business formation.

One phenomenon of both the recession and the recovery has been an increasing equalization of regional trends in business formation, as evidenced by recent slowdowns in business formation in Western and Southwestern states that had higher rates of new business formation between 1976 and 1980.[7]

TECHNIQUES AND TOOLS OF ECONOMIC DEVELOPMENT

States respond differently to the needs of various businesses. The following list highlights techniques and tools of economic development:

Direct financial incentives
    State-issued industrial revenue bonds
    Locally issued industrial revenue bonds
    State-issued general obligation bonds
    Locally issued general obligation bonds
    Umbrella bonds
    Industrial revenue bond guarantees
    Direct state loans
    Loan guarantees
    State-funded interest subsidies
    State-funded or state-chartered equity/venture
        capital corporations
    Privately sponsored development credit corporations
    Other financing programs
    Enterprise zones
    Customized industrial training

Tax exemptions, deductions, credits, and special treatment
    Job creation tax credit
    Investment tax credit
    Property tax abatement
    Business inventory
    Goods in transit
    Research and development
    Pollution control equipment
    Industrial machinery and equipment
    Industrial fuels and raw materials
    Energy and fuel conservation measures
    Other

Nonfinancial assistance
    Business consulting
        Management training

Market studies
Site selection
Licensing, regulation, and issuing of permits
Job training
Research and development
Business procurement assistance
Specialty services

Improvement of the business environment
Physical environment
Public infrastructure development
Land banking
Buildings
Business councils and economic development corporations

Source: Compiled from Urban Institute, *Directory of Incentives for Business Investment and Development in the U.S.* (Washington, D.C.: Urban Institute Press, 1983), Tables 1 and 4.

Parallel with the above programs, states have used incentive programs and have created promotional offices at home and abroad to entice non-U.S. MNCs to invest directly in their states (see Chapter 8). To encourage reverse or inward investment, states have also made concessions to foreign investors. Reverse licensing could provide the states with similar benefits without concessions. (We discuss this in detail in Chapter 3.) The literature on foreign direct investment (FDI) in the United States is relatively rich, and many scholars have investigated various aspects of FDI.[8]

Reverse licensing as an international sourcing strategy can help small and medium-sized manufacturing firms to survive. It can provide them with opportunities for access to new and competitive technology that would not be possible otherwise. In some cases, new and competitive foreign technology has resulted in the creation of new businesses in the United States. Masstron Scale, Inc., of Columbus, Ohio, is a unique example of the ways and means by which U.S. corporations have utilized foreign sources of technology. It also shows how reverse licensing could accomplish what reverse investment incentive programs are designed to do.

Reverse licensing can help small and medium-sized foreign firms to reach the U.S. market, a possibility not available otherwise. With the revenues from licensing contracts, these firms can expand their research and development (R&D) activities and, in some cases, survive.

THE MASSTRON SCALE, INC., CASE

Masstron is a relatively small high-tech scale company headquartered in Columbus, Ohio, that was established in 1978 when a licensing agreement was signed with a Swedish licensor. In 1984 Masstron employed about 77 and had annual sales of $20-25 million with $1-5 million in exports. Masstron has certain characteristics that make it different from other Ohio licensees:

1. The company was established because the licensor's executives knew Ben Dillon, president and founder of Masstron, personally (a case not predicted by our research hypotheses and questionnaire).

2. Masstron receives state-of-art technology from the licensor (a situation not expected of small and newly established firms and contrary to the established international business theories (FDI), in which the proprietor of technology licenses its new technology to another firm [especially if that firm is in the large U.S. market]). This case supports our argument that there are many small foreign firms with potentially good technology that are very anxious to reach the U.S. market but lack financial resources. Reverse licensing is the best alternative (perhaps the only one) available to them.

3. In 1982, after only four years, Masstron not only opened subsidiaries in Canada but had many advancements on the licensed technology and renegotiated the agreement with the licensor. Since then, because of cross-licensing arrangements, not only does Masstron have access to new developments by the licensor but it does not have to pay any licensing fees.

4. In late 1984, Masstron was about to sign new contracts with licensees in Brazil and the People's Republic of China (sublicense).

Without the U.S. market and similar sources of income, they would be in no better shape than their U.S. counterparts.

Small and medium-sized firms will play an even more important role in the U.S. economy. They are expected to grow at approximately 5 percent during 1985 and in the near future. Their share of overall employment gains is expected to be more than 25 percent, compared with approximately 2 percent for the larger enterprises. With their growth there will be even more business failures and bankruptcies. Reverse licensing could provide them with a mechanism to exploit foreign sources of technology.

In summary, reverse licensing is a mechanism for matching foreign (supply) with U.S. need for technology (demand), a mechanism that would provide U.S. manufacturing firms (particularly small and medium-sized ones) with new and competitive sources of technology not possible otherwise. Similarly, it provides the foreign firms (especially small and medium-sized ones) with the possibilities of reaching the U.S. market. Of course, the benefits are not limited to these groups. Reverse licensing is an international marketing (sourcing) strategy that can be used (and has been used) not only by U.S. MNCs but also in Japan and other industrialized nations. For decades, the Japanese have acquired most of their technological base and competitiveness through international licensing. Their international success may be attributable to their dependence on the import of foreign technology—they are net importers.

The problem to be studied is, therefore, evaluating the viability of reverse licensing as an alternative growth route for the survival of small and medium-sized U.S. manufacturing firms whose products are reaching the end of their PLC.

ORGANIZATION OF THE BOOK

This book is both theoretical and empirical. In Chapters 2–4, a theoretical model is developed and research hypotheses are proposed. In Chapters 5–7, the research model and hypotheses are empirically tested.

The importance of the United States in the international arena in general and in the licensing of technology in particular is discussed first. The historical role of the United States and the factors contributing to its deteriorating position in the international markets are also discussed. This sets the stage for a better understanding of the contributing factors, the relative shifts in the international industrial base, and the type of technology transferred. After a grasp of the macro picture, the research will focus on more specific cases of technology transfers.

In Chapter 2, the importance of technology licensing in general and of reverse licensing in particular is explained. International comparisons of R&D expenditures and activities, patenting, GNP growth rates, and licensing fees and royalties are made. The implications of these factors and their relevance to reverse licensing are explained.

In Chapter 3, the internationalization process of technology is discussed to see where licensing fits in. After defining technology transfer, types of transfers, and modes of transfer, the pros and cons of taking a license are evaluated. Then, licensing motivations from licensors' as well as licensees' points of view and other licensing issues are explained; the focus will be on reverse licensing and its comparison with reverse investment. The chapter concludes by discussing licensing benefits and how state governments should perceive reverse licensing.

In Chapter 4, a review of technology transfer and technology licensing literature is presented. The literature on technology licensing is relatively rich, but almost all of it has taken the licensor's standpoint—the opposite side of what this book is all about.

Chapter 5 builds upon the preceding chapters. First the research model is introduced. Then the net present value (NPV) technique is utilized in international technology licensing decisions from a licensee's point of view. Next, the licensing cycle model (LCM) and strategies for future technological needs are introduced. Finally, the study focuses on licensees' characteristics (size, R&D and technical competence, dominance), characteristics of licensed technology, and types of license agreements. Then the research hypotheses are proposed.

In Chapter 6, the model and research hypotheses are put to work. The hypotheses are operationalized to develop the research design, methodology, research instrument (questionnaire), and statistical design. The research focus is on 118 Ohio licensees as the sample for carrying out the empirical work. A discussion of how the questionnaire was designed is followed by a pilot study to test the reliability and validity of the research instrument.

In Chapter 7, the focus is on research results and statistical analyses. First is a discussion of how the research was carried out and how licensees responded to the questionnaire, followed by the researcher's interviews with licensees' executives. The hypotheses are tested using chi-square (χ^2) and gamma test statistics. Analyses and interpretations of the data and statistical testing are presented. The hypotheses and statistical analyses of the questionnaire are compared with the results of the interviews with the licensees' executives. The empirical findings and those not predicted by the research hypotheses and questionnaire conclude the chapter.

Chapter 8 summarizes the preceding chapters and concludes the study. A discussion of the limitations and the implications of the study is presented. The chapter ends with recommendations for future research in international technology transfer and technology licensing.

2

The International Setting
and the U.S. Position

This chapter consists of three interrelated parts. The first is a historical analysis of the U.S. international position. The second focuses on factors contributing to the deteriorating position of the United States since World War II. The final focus is on international patenting and technology licensing activities.

Following World War II, the United States dominated international business and transfer of technology. This dominant role began a downward trend with the rebirth of western Europe and Japan in the late 1950s to mid-1960s. The slower growth rate in the United States and higher growth rates in other industrialized countries had a doubly downward impact on the international position of the United States.

Factors responsible for such deterioration are basically science- and technology-related. The first and foremost is comparative levels of R&D activities. The second, which is directly related to R&D, is comparative number of patents and innovations. The third is U.S. international licensing activities.

Generally, R&D activities, patents and innovations, and licensing activities are interrelated, and expectations are that the higher the R&D activities, the higher the patents and innovations. Also, the higher the first two, the higher the international technology transfers.

THE U.S. INTERNATIONAL POSITION

Because of the enormous technological lead of the United States in the 1950s and 1960s, U.S. MNCs had a dominant role in R&D activities and the international transfer of U.S. technology. They have followed a practice of FDI in some foreign markets and licensing in others. Some firms, such as Westinghouse, have avoided FDI and have exploited international markets through a combination of licensing and exporting.

The dominant role of the United States in R&D began a downward trend in the 1960s and 1970s. In 1979 the United States had more scientists and engineers actively involved in R&D than France, West Germany, and Japan combined. It had 66 percent of all R&D scientists and engineers in industrialized countries in 1969; ten years later its share was 57 percent.[1]

FACTORS RESPONSIBLE FOR THE DETERIORATING U.S. POSITION

R&D and Science Factors

Since the mid-1960s, many of the leading industrialized countries have increased their investments in R&D relative to the United States. The growth rate of their R&D spending as a percentage of their GNP has surpassed that of the United States. West Germany has spent more than the United States, and Japan has closed the R&D gap (see Table 2.1).

An examination of annual growth rates of national R&D expenditures in constant terms shows that the United States lagged behind most other countries during the 1970s. In the mid- to late-1970s, the U.S. growth rate of R&D expenditures in real dollars averaged 2 percent, compared with 6 percent for Japan and 4 percent for West Germany.[2]

A closer look at the above statistics indicates that all countries except the United States increased their R&D spendings during 1961–82. In fact, U.S. spending declined by 5.5 percent, whereas during the same period, West Germany and Japan had the highest growth rates (114 percent and 100 percent, respectively).

Since the mid-1970s the import share of U.S. consumption has risen, and from 1970 to 1980 the U.S. market share in highly R&D-intensive industrial products declined (aircraft, 12.9 percent; electronics, 12.2 percent; jet engines, 8.4 percent).[3] Recent U.S. balance of payments statistics show that the trade deficit for 1985 was more than $120 billion. U.S. trade with West Germany has shown a deficit in chemicals and machinery products and equipment. The negative balance with Japan began to worsen in 1974.

TABLE 2.1 Estimated Nondefense R&D Expenditures as a Percent of GNP, by Country: 1971-85

Year	France	West Germany	Japan	United Kingdom	United States
1971	1.46	2.03	1.84	NA	1.68
1972	1.50	2.08	1.84	1.50	1.63
1973	1.38	1.94	1.89	NA	1.62
1974	1.43	1.98	1.96	NA	1.69
1975	1.46	2.08	1.95	1.41	1.68
1976	1.44	2.01	1.94	NA	1.68
1977	1.44	2.01	1.92	NA	1.67
1978	1.41	2.10	1.98	1.51	1.69
1979	1.42	2.27	2.08	NA	1.75
1980	1.43	2.30	2.21	NA	1.86
1981	1.51	2.38	2.37	1.72	1.87
1982 (prel.)	1.63	2.48	2.46	NA	1.94
1983 (est.)	1.69	2.47	2.60	1.61	1.91
1984 (est.)	1.76	NA	NA	NA	1.86
1985 (est.)	NA	NA	NA	NA	1.89

Source: National Science Foundation, National Science Board, Science Indicators 1985 (Washington, D.C.: U.S. Government Printing Office, 1986), p. 190.

By 1978, the deficit in R&D-intensive products was $5.7 billion—ten times what it had been in 1974.[4] Table 2.2 shows the overall U.S. trade balance in high-technology and other manufacturing products for 1975–84.

The losses in the U.S. market share were gained largely by Japan, West Germany, and France. A comparison of the world export shares of R&D-intensive products shows that the U.S. share declined from 35 percent in 1955 to 19 percent in 1980, while the combined share of Japan, West Germany, and France increased from about 20 percent to 43 percent during the same period.

Productivity in Manufacturing—An
International Comparison

Productivity growth in the economy in general and in the manufacturing sector in particular is directly related to R&D

TABLE 2.2 U.S. Trade in High-Technology and Other Manufacturing Product Groups: 1975-84 (billion constant 1972 dollars)

	High Technology			Nonhigh Technology		
	Exports	Imports	Balance	Exports	Imports	Balance
1975	18.20	7.55	10.65	38.24	36.17	2.07
1976	19.34	9.97	9.37	38.99	42.62	-3.63
1977	19.49	10.92	8.57	37.77	47.55	-9.78
1978	22.93	13.34	9.59	39.58	57.63	-18.06
1979	26.39	13.76	12.63	47.68	58.96	-11.27
1980	30.40	15.52	14.88	53.24	58.39	-5.15
1981	30.60	17.12	13.49	51.46	59.14	-7.68
1982 (est.)	27.75	16.45	11.31	43.31	56.19	-12.88
1983 (est.)	27.70	18.97	8.73	37.11	60.32	-23.21
1984 (est.)	29.08	26.29	2.79	38.59	77.53	-38.94

Source: National Science Foundations, National Science Board, Science Indicators 1985 (Washington, D.C.: U.S. Government Printing Office, 1986), p. 198.

spending, and is another important factor contributing to the international competitiveness of a country. The United States has lagged behind most of other industrialized countries during the past two decades.

Table 2.3 shows the productivity growth in manufacturing industries and labor costs for selected countries during 1973–84.

Productivity as measured by output per employee/hour in U.S. manufacturing leaped sharply upward in the year ending in 1983, the most recent one for which data are available. The rise exceeded that of any year back to 1950 except 1962–63, when a rise of more than 7 percent was recorded. A crucial factor will be the pace at which manufacturing output continues to expand.

As a result of the sharp jump in U.S. productivity, it held second place in the ranking of the seven major manufacturing countries in the world. By contrast, it was next to last in the year ending in 1982 and in the period 1973–83.[5]

Finally, a comparison of real gross domestic product (GDP) per employee indicates that the gap which existed between the United States and other industrialized nations

TABLE 2.3 Manufacturing Productivity and Labor Costs in Six Countries: Average Annual Rates of Change, 1973-84 (percent)

Country	Output per Man-hour			Hourly Compensation		
	1973-84	1983	1984	1973-84	1983	1984
United States	2.0	4.3	3.5	8.8	3.4	3.6
Canada	1.7	6.4	4.0	11.0	6.8	1.6
Japan	7.3	5.1	9.5	8.1	3.4	3.2
France	4.6	4.3	5.0	15.1	12.2	8.9
Germany	3.3	4.7	4.7	7.6	4.1	3.6
United Kingdom	2.3	6.7	3.9	15.9	7.2	7.9

	Unit Labor Costs in National Currency			Unit Labor Costs in U.S. Dollars		
	1973-84	1983	1984	1973-84	1983	1984
United States	6.7	-0.8	0.1	6.7	-0.8	0.1
Canada	9.2	.3	-2.3	6.3	.5	-7.0
Japan	.8	-1.7	-5.8	3.1	3.1	-5.7
France	10.0	7.6	3.7	4.5	-7.1	-9.5
Germany	4.1	-.5	-1.0	4.4	-5.4	-11.2
United Kingdom	13.4	.5	3.8	9.2	-12.9	-8.4

Note: Although the productivity measure relates output to the hours of persons employed in manufacturing, it does not measure the specific contributions of labor as a single factor of production. Rather, it reflects the joint effects of many influences, including new technology, capital investment, capacity utilization, energy use, and managerial skills, as well as the skills and efforts of the work force.

Source: U.S. Department of Labor, Bureau of Labor Statistics, 1986 U.S. Industrial Outlook (Washington, D.C.: U.S. Government Printing Office, 1986), p. 27.

in the 1950s has narrowed greatly. For instance, Japan's real GDP as a percent of U.S. GDP increased from 17.5 percent in 1950 to almost 74 percent in 1983—321 percent increase (see Table 2.4).

TABLE 2.4   Real Gross Domestic Product Per Employed Person, Selected
Countries, Compared With the United States: 1950-83 (United States = 100)

Year	United States	France	West Germany	Japan	United Kingdom	Canada
1950	100	43.9	39.6	17.5	53.1	84.3
1955	100	47.0	47.7	21.1	51.9	87.6
1960	100	55.7	60.2	26.9	53.7	88.1
1965	100	62.0	64.0	34.9	51.8	87.1
1970	100	73.5	75.0	52.0	56.5	91.9
1980	100	93.2	92.4	70.9	62.3	94.0
1981	100	93.5	92.4	72.5	62.8	94.3
1982	100	92.7	93.8	74.2	65.7	93.5
1983	100	94.3	93.8	73.7	66.0	92.0

Note: Output is based on international price weights to enable cross-
country comparisons.
   Source: National Science Foundation, National Science Board, Science
Indicators 1985 (Washington, D.C.: U.S. Government Printing Office, 1985),
p. 196.

Patents—An International Comparison

Patents granted are another indicator of a country's R&D
spending and technological competitiveness.   In terms of
total number of patents, western Europe combined had
33,927 new patents in 1973 and 73,337 in 1983 (+116 percent).   The numbers for Japan were 18,410 in 1973 and
54,701 in 1983 (+197 percent).   The number of patents in
the United States was 74,139 in 1973; it declined to 56,862
in 1983 (-30 percent).[6]
   A breakdown of the total number of patents by nationality of inventors for the United States, western Europe,
and Japan is perhaps more meaningful.   Table 2.5 shows
patents granted in selected countries by nationality of
inventors during 1972–82.   During this period, patents
granted in the United States to U.S. nationals declined from
51,515 in 1972 to 37,152 in 1980 (-28 percent), and in western Europe patents granted to the individual country nationals declined from 20,409 to 18,264 (-10.5 percent).   In
Japan, on the other hand, patents granted to Japanese
nationals increased from 29,101 in 1972 to 38,032 in 1980 (31
percent).

TABLE 2.5 Patents Granted in Selected Countries, by Nationality of Inventors, 1972-82

	U.S.			Japan			West Germany			France		
	Total	Natls.	Forgnrs.	Total	Natls.	Forgnrs.	Total	Natl.	Forgnrs.	Total	Natls.	Forgnrs.
1972	74,808	51,515	23,293	41,545	29,101	12,353	20,600	9,642	10,958	46,217	10,767	35,450
1974	76,275	50,643	25,634	39,626	30,873	8,753	20,539	9,793	10,746	24,725	9,282	15,443
1976	70,236	44,162	26,074	40,317	32,465	7,852	20,965	10,395	10,570	29,754	8,420	21,334
1978	66,102	40,979	25,123	45,504	37,648	7,856	23,514	11,581	11,933	30,530	8,083	22,447
1980	61,827	37,152	24,675	46,106	38,032	8,074	20,188	9,826	10,362	28,060	8,438	19,622
1981-82	222,843	NA	NA	205,113	NA	NA	NA	NA	NA	45,516	NA	NA

Natls. = Nationals
Forgnrs. = Foreigners

Source: Compiled from National Science Foundation, National Science Board, Science Indicators 1982 (Washington, D.C.: U.S. Government Printing Office, 1984) and Science Indicators 1985 (Washington, D.C.: U.S. Government Printing Office, 1986); World Intellectual Property Organization.

During the same period, foreign patents granted to U.S. nationals numbered 48,807 in 1972, declining to 31,301 in 1980 (-36 percent). On the other hand, U.S. patents granted to foreign nationals increased from 23,293 to 24,675 (6 percent). If patents are any indicators of a country's degree of inventiveness, the United States has become relatively less inventive compared, at least, with Japan.

One implication of such patenting activities is that U.S. corporations can utilize foreign patents as another source of new technology. Even though the number of patents has declined in western Europe, the 18,264 patents granted to nationals in 1980 is a fairly large source of new technology. When one adds this to 38,032 patents granted to nationals in Japan in 1980, it becomes apparent that foreign sources of new technology are just over 150 percent more than U.S. sources (56,296 for western Europe and Japan combines, as opposed to 37,152 for the United States in 1980).

As noted above, U.S. patents granted to foreign nationals showed an increase of 6 percent between 1972 and 1980. This means that foreign inventors are becoming more interested in exploiting the U.S. market, and for that reason they protect their inventions and property rights in the United States. U.S. firms could utilize these sources that have already indicated interest in entering the U.S. market.

Various factors influence the level of patenting activities in different industries and different countries. High-tech status, maturity, and the level of innovations as opposed to patents are among the factors having direct impact. Other factors affect patenting activities, and there are various explanations for the existence of the above patterns.

Perhaps U.S. corporations have been more inclined to use trade secrets and innovations instead of patenting. However, the propensity to use patents or trade secrets differs among industries, firms, and inventions:

> The propensity to patent is highest in industries, such as the drug industry, where technical advances can be easily copied by competitors, and lowest where they are technically difficult to imitate or where technological advances occur very rapidly. Therefore, one would expect that trends in patenting activity would vary among industries and product fields. However, this does not seem to be the case. Patenting activity by U.S. inventors has decreased in almost all product fields, and therefore, the U.S. drop in patenting may actually

indicate a decrease in the production rate of U.S. inventions rather than being primarily attributable to increased use of trade secrets.[7]

The pattern of industrial R&D activities in industrially developed countries varies; they have greater or lesser emphasis on industrial R&D or defense-related R&D. While the United States, England, and France have given a higher priority to defense-related R&D, Japan and West Germany have spent more on industrial R&D.

Finally, the status of an industry (R&D-intensive or non-R&D-intensive) and its maturity are also determinants of patenting activities (see Figures 2.1 and 2.2).

Figure 2.1 Patent Statistics as Technology Indicators: High-tech Status of Industries

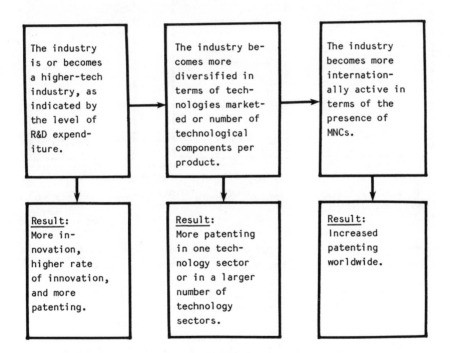

Source: J. J. Franklin, "Patent Statistics as Technology Indicators" (M.S. thesis, Georgia Institute of Technology, 1983), p. 16.

It was indicated earlier that foreigners have increased their patenting activities in the United States. This is

Figure 2.2 Patent Statistics as Technology Indicators:
Industry Maturity

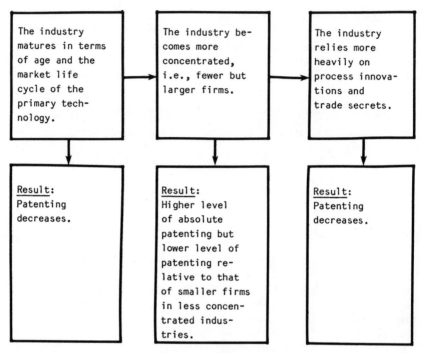

Source: J. J. Franklin, "Patent Statistics as Technology
Indicators" (M.S. thesis, Georgia Institute of Technology,
1983), p. 16.

partially because of certain characteristics of the U.S.
market, including market pull and technology push:

> Perhaps economic promise is a strong determinant
> . . . of the level of foreign patenting in general,
> while technological inventiveness determines product
> areas in which foreign patenting occurs.
> In the period 1979–1981, in each of the four
> different product fields—medicines, primary metals,
> aircraft and parts (including engines and turbines),
> and textile mill products—almost half of all U.S.
> patents were granted to foreign nationals. Foreign
> inventors were granted 40 percent or more of the
> U.S. patents in four additional fields. Some of
> these foreign patents are assigned to U.S. organ-

izations or individuals. For example, although 49 percent of all U.S. patents in the field of drugs and medicines are granted to foreign inventors, 14 percent of these foreign-origin patents are actually owned by U.S. entities. U.S. ownership of foreign-origin patents is significant in the product fields of chemicals, drugs, communication equipment, and petroleum and natural gas. It is very possible that U.S. research efforts abroad produced many of these patented inventions and that they are produced by foreigners working for U.S. firms.[8]

U.S. International Technology Licensing

Finally, to show the significance of international licensing of technology and its importance to the United States, this book looks at U.S. international transactions of royalties and fees. In 1983, the total amount of such transactions (receipts and payments) was $8.3 billion, of which $7.85 billion was U.S. receipts of royalties and fees.[9] The statistics published by the U.S. Department of Commerce are the only publicly available information on international licensing of technology. They clearly indicate the importance of U.S. MNCs as licensors in the international transfer of technology (see Table 2.6). Also, internal technology transfers (from U.S. parents to foreign affiliates), as opposed to external transfers (from U.S. corporations to unaffiliated foreign corporations), is significant.

Historically, the ratio of royalties and fees (unaffiliated/affiliated receipts) has been low and constant (approximately 25 percent) in the United States (see Table 2.7). However, the ratio of payments by U.S. firms during 1975–83 was 1.15 (115 percent). One implication is that during that period, payments by U.S. corporations grew faster than their receipts. This indicates that U.S. firms are buying more technology through licensing arrangements from unaffiliated foreign corporations. During 1982 and 1983 the growth rates of these payments were 370 percent and 165 percent, respectively.

The U.S. corporations involved in international licensing of technology were receiving about one-fourth of their royalties and fees from unaffiliated sources. They were paying three times higher than their foreign counterparts. If these ratios are used as indicators of licensing activities, it becomes clear that most of the U.S. firms' licensing operations (as licensor) are with their affiliates in foreign countries. During 1975–83, payments by U.S. licensees to

TABLE 2.6 U.S. International Transactions of Royalties and Fees, 1976–85 (million dollars)

	1976	1977	1978	1979	1980	1981	1982	1983	1984	1985
Receipts										
Fees & royalties from affiliated foreigners	3,531	3,883	4,705	4,980	5,780	5,794	5,561	6,275	6,530	4,980
Fees & royalties from unaffiliated foreigners	822	1,037	1,180	1,204	1,305	1,490	1,572	1,579	1,585	1,265
Total	4,353	4,920	5,885	6,184	7,085	7,284	7,133	7,854	8,115	
Annual growth rate (%)	1.2	13.0	19.6	5.0	14.6	2.8	2.0	10.0	3.3	
Payments										
Fees & royalties to affiliated foreigners	-293	-243	-393	-523	-428	-435	-72	-170	-187	-141
Fees & royalties to unaffiliated foreigners	-189	-262	-277	-309	-297	-289	-267	-282	-329	-273
Total	-482	-505	-670	-832	-725	-724	-339	-452	-516	
Annual growth rate (%)	1.9	4.7	32.6	24.2	12.8	0.0	-53.0	33.5	14.2	
Total receipts & payments	4,835	5,425	6,555	7,016	7,810	8,008	7,472	8,306	8,631	

Note: 1985 data are for three quarters only.
Source: Compiled from various issues of Survey of Current Business, published by U.S. Department of Commerce.

unaffiliated licensors were greater than payments by U.S. licensees to their foreign affiliates.

THE GAP BETWEEN PATENTING AND LICENSING ACTIVITIES

A closer look at patenting activities shows that the United States, western Europe, and Japan have approximately equal patenting activities and that almost half of U.S. patents have been granted to foreign inventors. If patents are indicators of a country's degree of inventiveness and technological advancement, then logically one would expect to see more of a balance in international technology transactions. This means that the ratio of U.S. payments to receipts of royalties and fees (unaffiliated) should be approaching unity. With western Europe and Japan gaining in patenting activities and with the United States losing, the U.S. payments should be increasing at a faster rate than receipts. The U.S. Department of Commerce data do not show such a trend. In fact, the ratio of payments to receipts (unaffiliated) for the United States during 1977–85 decreased from 25 percent to 21 percent. Also the overall ratio of U.S. payments to receipts declined from 10 percent to 6 percent during 1977–85 (see Table 2.8).

One explanation of such a contradiction might be related to the fact that U.S. corporations are not utilizing foreign sources of technology to the extent that they should. This, in turn, might be due to various reasons: (1) U.S. ignorance of such foreign sources; (2) absence of a mechanism to increase U.S. awareness and to facilitate the reverse transfer of technology; (3) other countries have grown faster than the United States, but not enough to close the gap; (4) FDI in the United States, which has increased greatly in recent years. U.S. Department of Commerce data do not show that any of these is the case.

TAPPING SOVIET BLOC TECHNOLOGY

MNCs have been scanning international markets on a continuing basis and have acquired patents and know-how from foreign licensors. These U.S. licensees have not limited themselves to U.S. allies as foreign sources of technology. They have actively sought and acquired technology from Communist bloc countries, especially the USSR and the German Democratic Republic. A case in point is Trident Motors of Columbus, Ohio.

TABLE 2.7 U.S. Receipts and Payments of Royalties and Fees, 1976-85 (unaffiliated/affiliated ratio)

	1976	1977	1978	1979	1980	1981	1982	1983	1984	1985
Receipts	.23	.27	.25	.24	.23	.26	.28	.25	.24	.25
Payments	.64	1.08	.70	.59	.69	.66	3.7	1.65	1.76	1.93

Receipts--annual average ration 1976-85: .246
Payments--annual average ratio 1976-85: 1.290

Source: Calculated by author from various issues of Survey of Current Business, published by U.S. Department of Commerce.

TABLE 2.8 U.S. Payments/Receipts of Royalties and Fees: 1977-85

	1977	1978	1979	1980	1981	1982	1983	1984	1985
Payments/receipts (affiliated)	.06	.08	.10	.07	.07	.01	.03	.03	.03
Payments/receipts (unaffiliated)	.25	.23	.25	.23	.20	.17	.18	.20	.21
Payments/receipts (total)	.10	.11	.13	.10	.10	.05	.05	.06	NA

Source: Calculated by author from various issues of Survey of Current Business, published by U.S. Department of Commerce.

THE TRIDENT MOTORS COMPANY CASE

Trident Motors is a small vehicle manufacturer in Columbus, Ohio. The Company recently signed a contract to assemble and distribute a small, multi-purpose truck built by a state-owned East German company. The agreement is very significant because it represents the first ever joint manufacturing effort in the United States between the Communist-bloc nation and an American company.

According to Denny Vincent, Trident's vice-president, the Company should be able to eventually manufacture the truck with Ohio-built parts and create 300 to 500 jobs by the end of the 1980s.

The Ohio Department of Development's International Trade Division was instrumental in introducing the German company to Trident. The Department earlier had introduced Trident to a light-weight British engine for a three-wheeled truckster used for refuse collection, grounds maintenance, and by police departments.

Trident estimates that approximately 3,000 trucks a year will be sold by 1989 and the truck will be very popular because it is very economical (approximately $24,000) and does more functions than existing large dump trucks. The German truck will do a variety of functions year-round, and various municipalities with budgetary constraints would be able to save tremendously.

The East German truck is widely sold throughout Europe and highly regarded for its compact size, maneuverability, and ability to perform a number of tasks such as plowing snow, hauling refuse, and spreading gravel.

Source: The Trident Company.

Table 2.8 lists active Soviet licenses in the U.S. Some of the technology acquired from the Eastern bloc is being developed for military applications in addition to commercial applications:

Soviet technology acquired by several U.S. companies in the 1970's, mainly through technical exchanges, is just now being developed for a variety of U.S. military applications. These range from improved armored vehicles and jet fighter engines to better radar equipment, communication systems and even beam weapons.[10]

The above statistics not only show the importance of international transfer of technology, but are alarming to

TABLE 2.8 Active Soviet Licenses in the United States

Technology	Sold To	Approx. Date
Surgical stapling instruments	U.S. Surgical Corp./3M	1964
Hydraulic rock crusher	Joy Manufacturing	1969
Pneumatic underground punch ("hole hog")	Allied Steel & Tractor	1971
Evaporative stave cooling of blast furnaces	Andco Eng.	1972
Aluminum silicon alloy	Ethyl Corp.	1973
Production of hollow ingots by electroslage remelting	Cabot	1973
Flux cored electrodes	Chemetron	1974
Magnetic impact bonding	Maxwell Lab.	1974
Drug pyrroxan for treating central nervous system disorders	American Home Products	1974
Ethnozin for treating cardiac arrest	Dupont	1974
Electromagnetic casting of aluminum	Kaiser Aluminum Reynolds Aluminum Alcoa	1975
Carboxide insect repellant	American Home Products	1975
In situ underground coal gasification	Texas Utilities Services	1975
Carminomycin and Florafur anti-cancer agents	Bristol Myers	1976
Bulat process for titanium nitriding	Multiarc Vacuum Systems	1979
Flash butt welding of large-diameter pipes	J. R. McDermott	1980
Electromagnetic casting of copper alloys	Olin Brass	1980
Cone crusher	Rexnord	1981
Air column separator	Air Products	1981
Medical preparation riocidin	Ciba Geigy USA	1982
Biodegradable polymer pin for orthopedics	Medo	1982

Source: John W. Kiser III, "Tapping Soviet Technology," in Common Sense in U.S.-Soviet Trade (American Committee on East-West Trade, Washington, D.C. 1983), p. 106.

U.S. businesses and government bodies because of the impact that such diffusion has on future U.S. competitiveness and industrial technology. Equally important is the effect of the deterioration of U.S. technology on national security and technological dependence.

SUMMARY

To summarize, the postwar dominant role of the United States in international business and transfer of technology began to deteriorate in the late 1950s and 1960s. Various factors were responsible for such deterioration:

1. The decline of the U.S. share of world scientists and engineers (from 66 percent in 1969 to 57 percent in 1979)
2. The growth rate in R&D by other industrialized countries surpassed that of the United States in many cases
3. The shift in the world industrial structure and relative growth of other industrialized countries relative to that of the United States
4. The productivity growth in U.S. manufacturing industries deteriorated relative to other industrialized countries
5. A sharp increase in the patenting activities of other industrialized countries (197 percent for Japan) and a sharp decline for the United States (-40 percent)[11]
6. A comparison of the ratio of licensing receipts and payments, and of international patenting activities, indicates that U.S. corporations are not utilizing foreign patents and technology to the extent that they should
7. The changes in the ratio of unaffiliated/affiliated receipts and payments of fees and royalties indicate that U.S. corporations bought more technology from unaffiliated sources than they sold to unaffiliated sources during 1977–85
8. Scientific and technological cooperation between U.S. corporations and the Soviet Union and other Eastern bloc countries has resulted in more licensing activities by U.S. MNCs utilizing Soviet bloc technology.

Chapter 3 concerns the internationalization of business, with particular focus on licensing. The cases for and against licensing, licensing motivations, and a comparison of reverse licensing with reverse investment are among the topics covered.

3

International Technology Licensing

In Chapter 2, the international licensing position of the United States was examined and the factors contributing to its deterioration were evaluated. The statistics showed that there was a contradiction between international patenting activities and international licensing fees and royalties in the United States.

The contradiction arose when it was shown that other developed countries had surpassed the United States in terms of patenting activities, which implies a significant increase in the flow of technology into the United States. However, the data on licensing fees and royalties did not support the expectations. It was concluded that perhaps the ignorance of U.S. corporations about foreign technology and/or the absence of a mechanism for facilitating the flow of technology to the United States were among the reasons for such a contradiction.

In this chapter, types of technology transfer mechanisms and the internationalization of technology are defined. Then, licensing motivations and the cases for and against technology licensing from the licensees' point of view, and licensing issues are discussed. Finally, reverse licensing and reverse investment are compared and contrasted, and reverse licensing benefits are analyzed from three different standpoints: U.S. licensees, foreign licensors, and the public sector.

TECHNOLOGY TRANSFER: DEFINITION

Technology is a perishable resource comprising knowledge, skills, and the means for using and controlling factors of production for the purpose of producing, delivering to users, and maintaining goods and services for which there is an economic and/or social demand.[1]

Technology is to be distinguished from science. Science organizes and explains data and observations by means of theoretical relationships, whereas technology translates scientific and empirical relationships into practical use.[2]

In order to get a clear picture of technology transfer and to see the stages through which an idea passes before it becomes a useful product or process, it is useful to inspect a scheme of technology transfer (see Figure 3.1).

Figure 3.1 M.I.T. Scheme of Technology Transfer

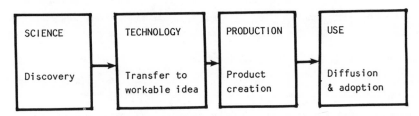

Source: J. Peter Killing, "Manufacturing Under License in Canada" (Ph.D. diss., University of Western Ontario, 1975), p. 26.

There are basically two types of technology flows or transfers; horizontal and vertical. The works of Morton and of Killing are of particular interest in this regard. Figure 3.2 shows both vertical and horizontal transfer of technology. Vertical transfer is within a firm, while horizontal transfer is inter-firm, between two separate entities. Vertical technology transfer takes place at three levels within a firm; from basic and applied research to development and design to manufacturing. Horizontal transfer takes place at three levels: science, technology, and production.

Technology Transfer at the Science Level

The transfer of technology at this level is the flow of scientific information between scientists and engineers (involved in R&D) of different firms. At this stage, abstract ideas are communicated by various means. Rosenbloom and Wolek, in a study of more than 3,000 scientists

Figure 3.2   Horizontal and Vertical Technology Transfer

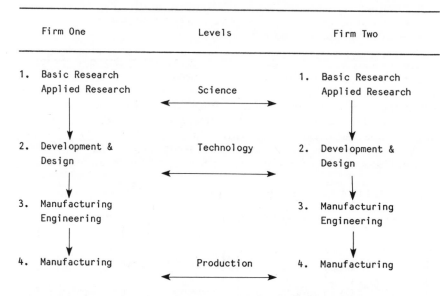

Source: J. Peter Killing, "Manufacturing Under License in Canada" (Ph.D. diss., University of Western Ontario, 1975), p. 28.

and engineers involved in R&D laboratories, found that professional journals, books, conferences, and conversations with fellow scientists were the means of communicating scientific information.[3]   At this stage, transfer of technology is not managed through license agreements because there is nothing to license.   The only way for a firm to become part of this process is to hire scientists and engineers capable of entering the dialogue:

> If you are to tap the world's science and technology you have to create some science.   Your admission ticket to the club is to have something of your own to talk about.

Technology Transfer at the Technology Level

This is the stage where workable ideas are put into commercially feasible applications.   The information flow is related to a product or process that has not been commercially proven.   At this stage, license agreements could be used for the transfer of technology.

If a firm is to receive information at this stage (as a licensee), it must have its own development, manufacturing, and marketing capabilities. Without them, the licensee would not be able to develop the product and introduce it into the market. Technology is not a self-contained physical object that is stored on a warehouse shelf and shipped as a package from the supplier to the user; it is a body of knowledge transferred by a learning process. When transfer is from one nation to another, it can be complex, time-consuming, and costly, even if it is between units of the same MNC. The time required, the costs, and the effectiveness of technology transfers will vary with such factors as the nature of the technology being transferred, and the characteristics, capabilities, and objectives of the parties involved.[4]

Technology Transfer at the Production Level

The technology transferred at this level is a commercially proven product or process. The recipient of the technology needs technical information (blueprints, engineering drawings, and such) to begin production. Most licensing agreements take place at this level. At this stage, the licensee understands the value of the technology that will be acquired, and enters the contract with some confidence. Even at this level, the licensee will need some engineering competence to evaluate the technology being offered and to adapt it to local conditions. The absorptive capability of the licensee is extremely important in the transfer process. The time required, the expenses, and the effectiveness of the technology transfer vary with the type of technology, the recipient's capabilities, and the relationship between the parties. A transfer of automobile technology from a Japanese firm to a U.S. firm could occur rapidly, effectively, and relatively inexpensively. A similar transfer to a company in a developing country (such as Mexico) with a limited supply of trained and experienced personnel could take a longer time and have a higher cost.

INTERNATIONALIZATION OF TECHNOLOGY

The proprietor of a technology has a monopolistic power over its firm-specific advantage (FSA). This advantage could be technology, marketing skills, or management know-how. Technology and its international transfer are defined later in the chapter. Here, the focus is on the

options available to the proprietor for exploiting the technology in the global markets. First, the owner might use
the technology by producing at home and exporting to other
markets. Traditionally, exporting is the least risky
alternative and the first step in the internationalization
process.

Second, the owner might utilize the technology by
producing for the global market in the global market. The
production decisions are made on an international re-
turn/risk trade-off. There will be various production
facilities around the world, and products reach consumers
through a multinational network. The risk associated with
this strategy (FDI) is perhaps the highest and, therefore,
the returns should be the highest—at least in theory. This
is possible because the proprietor can internalize all the
benefits of the technology or the firm-specific advantage.[5]

Allan Rugman et al. consider the proprietor of the FSA
to be a multinational enterprise (MNE) with monopolistic
characteristics. The advantage is assumed to be retained
within the MNE's organizational structure:

> The monopolistic nature of the firm-specific advan-
> tage leads, in theory, to excessive profits (or
> "rents"), but these are *reduced by special costs of
> alternative modes of servicing the foreign markets
> in which the MNE operates* [emphasis added].
> These special costs are inherent in running an
> internal market; so that the profits of the MNE are
> always smaller than they would be if an external
> market for the MNE's firm-specific advantage
> existed. . . . it is clear that the MNE's have many
> rivals, so they are really in a situation of mono-
> polistic competition. In such a market structure
> excess profits are eliminated by the actions of rival
> MNEs.[6]

Looking at the performance of the world's largest MNEs,
they find no evidence of excess profits. And, considering
the choices to be made by the MNE for the exploitation of
international markets, they argue that

> . . . the MNE runs the risk of dissipation of its
> firm-specific advantage if it engages in licensing,
> since the licensees may be able to resell information
> about the FSA of the MNE to outside parties or to
> use it themselves to compete against the MNE.[7]

Extending the Hirsch model to include licensing and the risk of dissipation, Rugman et al. use the following variables and notations to show MNEs' preference for international market exploitation modes:[8]

Country-Specific Costs

C = aggregate production function (home)

C^* = aggregate production function (foreign)

Special Costs

M^* = Export marketing costs (goods market)

A^* = Additional cost of FDI (goods and factor markets)

D^* = Risk of dissipation of FSA (risk of lost sales and costs of enforcement of licensing agreement).

The MNE has to choose among alternatives for servicing foreign markets:[9]

1. Export if $C + M^* < C^* + A^*$ (exporting is cheaper than FDI) and $C + M^* < C^* + D^*$ (exporting is cheaper than licensing).
2. FDI if $C^* + A^* < C + M^*$ (FDI is cheaper than exporting) and $C^* + A^* < C^* + D^*$ (FDI is cheaper than licensing).
3. License if $C^* + D^* < C^* + A^*$ (licensing costs are less than FDI) and $C^* + D^* < C + M^*$ (licensing costs are less than exporting).

Rugman et al. argue that if markets are perfect (no information cost or barriers to trade), exporting is the first option. If markets are imperfect (tariffs or other trade barriers exist) and if there is the risk of dissipation of FSA, foreign markets are best served through FDI. If such risks are nonexistent, but the host nation imposes regulations on the MNE that are greater than the benefits of FDI, then the MNE should license its FSA (technology) to a foreign licensee. The license fees are usually greater to the licensee than to MNE subsidiaries, because with the subsidiary such risks are nonexistent.[10]

The third option available to the owner is a joint venture. Even though the owner of technology wants exclusive exploitation of the technology (internalization or FDI), various barriers and regulations may force the owner into a joint-venture operation.

Fourth, licensing might be used to utilize the ownership-specific advantage (technology), by allowing the licensee to utilize the technology under certain conditions for a specific period of time, for a specified price (license fees or royalties). A subset of licensing strategy will be the focus of this research endeavor.

Finally, due to the complexities in international operations and various external as well as internal constraints on MNCs, a combination of various market entry strategies such as FDI, licensing, and international trades might be used.

THE INTERNATIONAL PRODUCT LIFE CYCLE

According to the international product life cycle (IPLC), a product is first introduced in the domestic market when the firm sees a demand for it. At this stage, the product may be unstandardized, the inputs may vary, and the manufacturing processes may fluctuate. Because of these uncertainties, the firm needs to be close to its customers, suppliers, and competitors. At the second stage, with increased production and overseas demand, the product is exported (usually to other developed countries). At the next stage, when the product is mature, the need for flexibility in the manufacturing process declines. The firm can make a long-term commitment because of reduced uncertainties, and with the economics of scale, product cost takes precedence over product characteristics. At the final stage, when the product is standardized because of overseas competition, multiple product facilities will be utilized. At this stage, because of cost considerations, the production will be shifted to less-developed countries (LDCs), where the costs are lowest. The investment in LDCs is usually seen as vertical integration in which the parent company (a U.S. firm) provides the inputs and buys the output for global distribution. The home market is now served through imports. The empirical test of IPLC for about 140 categories of nondurable consumer goods has found it to be generally valid.[11] This does not mean that international operations of MNEs generally follow the IPLC.

When the proprietor of a technology is a large firm, it has enough resources and expertise to exploit international markets by using export, FDI, and licensing. But when the proprietor is a small or medium-sized company with limited resources and perhaps limited international exposure, the opportunities for exploitation of international markets are also limited. Because of the firm's limited resources or international trade barriers, FDI and foreign sales offices could be ruled out. The only viable option open to the proprietor might be licensing of its technology. An appropriate foreign licensee could provide the small-to-medium-sized licensor with the opportunity to exploit overseas markets not otherwise available. Technology licensing therefore is one of the market entry strategies, though not the prime choice of MNCs unless all other preferred strategies are not available. Although many scholars (such as Rugman et al.) argue that licensing takes place only after other options are exhausted, there is no consensus on the sequence of events. Licensing might precede FDI, or exporting in an internationalization process.

MODES OF TECHNOLOGY LICENSING

Despite the motivations of licensors and licensees, there are basically four key modes for technology licensing.

1. Inventor–corporation. This is a case where the inventor/patent holder is an individual or a small firm. Because of a lack of financial resources, the inventor cannot exploit the invention commercially. Consequently, the invention must be licensed to a firm able to exploit it. In this situation, the licensee has complete control over manufacturing and marketing of the product and pays licensing fees to the licensor.

2. Corporation–corporation. This is the classic licensing situation in which a corporation licenses its technology (patent rights and in many cases technical know-how) to another corporation in exchange for a royalty (a percentage of the sales). In this case licensing is one of many options open to the licensor (others are joint venture and FDI). Perhaps the licensor chooses licensing because of a relatively low (or no) commitment of capital and management, and a relatively low (or no) political risk. The licensor's motivation is to increase its profitability and earn extra revenues by capitalizing its R&D competence. Of particular interest in this regard is Friedman and Kalmanoff's comment on Westinghouse's licensing program.

> Some companies, of which Westinghouse is a prime example, have specialized in licensing as the preferred form of joint venturing. The reason is the disinclination to commit large amounts of capital

abroad—especially in view of the capital-intensive nature of the industry and the high cost of new plants—and because of the research program being conducted. The research and development effort is so extensive and successful that Westinghouse can count on retaining a long lead in product development over its licensees, thereby minimizing the risk that the technology transferred will build a dangerous rival, or that the licensees will wish to terminate the relationship at the end of the licensing period.[12]

In some cases, licensing of technology may be the only way of entering a foreign market, particularly when more and more countries limit imports of foreign products and FDI.

The very carefully structured trade off analysis in international business texts is becoming increasingly obsolete as an ever larger number of countries decide that certain alternatives, such as direct investment, are not available to foreign firms. Regardless of its relative profitability, licensing is likely to become of increasing interest to firms wishing to enter foreign markets, because of the increasing nationalism in many countries.

3. Cross-licensing. This arrangement usually takes place between two firms of similar standing in terms of technological competence. The motivation here is more to have access to the new development of the licensed technology rather than royalty revenues. Instead of asking the licensee to pay for the technology, the licensee's R&D findings will be exchanged for new developments. Cross-licensing is widely practiced, particularly in industries (such as pharmaceuticals) where R&D costs are very high and technology is very advanced.

4. Interfirm licensing. This type of licensing arrangement is vertical, and the motivations vary with the circumstances. Interfirm licensing has become a common practice in MNCs. One motive might involve political risk in the host country of the MNC's subsidiary (for instance, control over transfers of certain types of funds). Other motives might be legal, financial (such as avoiding taxes), and/or allocation of the parent's R&D expenditures to its subsidiaries. This type of licensing is not central to this research.

LICENSING MOTIVATIONS

The motivations of licensors for licensing their technology are different from those of licensees. In this section, the technology licensing motivations are discussed from both licensors' and licensees' standpoints.

The Licensor

Licensors license their technology for various reasons: (1) to earn revenues not otherwise possible, (2) to extend the technology's life (declining in commercial use in the licensor's market), (3) to establish and/or test the market for future FDI, (4) to facilitate payment for use of the technology by the licensee where the recipient country has established limitations on transfer of dividends and (5) because of cross-licensing arrangements with the licensee.

Prior to licensing its technology, the licensor attempts to foresee all the issues and problems that might be raised through the licensing agreement. The field of use is one source of conflict between the licensor and the licensee; the licensee may use technology in fields not specified or paid for in the contract. Another is geographical restrictions (counter to antitrust laws of many countries); the licensee may exploit markets not included in the contract. Although the licensing agreement may have provisions for such occurrences, it is very difficult and costly to maintain full control and to police the licensed technology.

The creation of a competitor for the licensor is another disadvantage. The licensee will be competing with the licensor's product not only in the geographical location or markets covered in the contract but in other markets as well. This is an opportunity cost to the licensor, and must be considered in royalty and compensation arrangements. Although there may be provisions for such opportunity costs, the licensor cannot be fully compensated for the existence of new competition. Especially if the licensee achieves technical and marketing competence in conjunction with its other advantages (such as location-specific advantages), it becomes almost impossible for the licensor to compete with the licensee.

The Licensees

Very few scholars have investigated licensees' motivations for acquisition of technology through licensing arrangements. In this section, the licensees' motivations are central to the analysis. Bloxam and Killing argue that the main decision, from licensees' viewpoint, is whether to take a license. They summarize the cases for and against such action.[13]

The licensees' motivations for taking a license are essentially (1) to acquire the needed technology and/or to supplement their own in-house R&D activities; (2) to avoid R&D expenditures because of the presence of the probability of failure; (3) to acquire the right to operate or to settle a patent dispute—the licensee might have developed the technology independent of the licensor but because of the existence of a patent on the technology, it has to acquire a license; and (4) to get the technology (product) to the market faster—the licensee has the capability to develop the needed technology (product), but taking a license will expedite the manufacturing and marketing process.

The reasons not to take a license are (1) adaptation costs required to utilize the licensed technology; (2) opportunity costs resulting from lengthy negotiations; (3) lost advantages of strengthening a firm's own R&D and the "not invented here" (NIH) syndrome exhibited by a licensee's own R&D team; (4) the existing patent laws (weak versus strong law) and the ability of the recipient firm to build around the patented technology.

LICENSING ISSUES

The Negotiation Process

In order to reach a final agreement, licensor and licensee spend a fair amount of time in the negotiation process. Various issues and factors, such as legal considerations, pricing and compensation arrangements, the contractual agreement, and the licensor-licensee relationship and cooperation, are discussed and agreed upon. Negotiation on some of the issues will be smooth, but some issues will present difficulties to reaching (or trying to reach) a final agreement. Factors discussed during the negotiations may be financial, technical, legal, organizational, and governmental:

1. Financial factors include valuation of the technology, payment conditions (currency, financing, inflation), and financial participation by the licensor.
2. Technical factors include separation of the items of

the aggregate (unbundling), performance guarantees, adaptation and modification of technology, quality control, field of use, and cross-licensing arrangements.

3. Legal factors include applicable laws and arbitration provisions, the secrecy obligation of licensee, the scope of geographical rights, the duration of technical assistance to the licensee, and product liability.

4. Organizational and governmental factors include private negotiations between the parties involved, the home and host governments, and international organizations (the United Nations, the Paris Convention).

Compensation and Pricing

Each licensing agreement is unique. Compensation arrangements vary with the technology, the bargaining power of licensor and licensee, the duration of the contract, the amount of technical assistance provided, the geographical location, and the field of use of the licensed technology.

The compensation arrangements in international technology licensing may create conflict between the parties and the antitrust laws of the countries involved. The pricing arrangements (such as percentage of licensed technology sales or lump sum) have a direct bearing on the profitability of technology licensing for both parties. In other words, restrictions in the licensing package may change the technology transfer mechanism (such as FDI, licensing).[14]

Legal Considerations

Legal considerations play a vital role in technology licensing. The success or failure of a licensing agreement depends on the willingness of the licensor and the licensee, and the binding contract between them. In practice, the licensor owns some intellectual property (know-how) and is willing to sell (transfer) this property to the licensee. The licensee on the other had is willing to receive (acquire) the technology for a fee. Willingness and cooperation on the part of both parties are critically important. The legal arrangement that makes parties abide by their promises is the licensing agreement. The patent system, antitrust laws, and other legal considerations not part of this study are very important in international technology licensing.

Licensor-Licensee Relationship

The success or failure of technology licensing depends directly on the relationship between the parties. Prior to

licensing arrangements, the licensor and the licensee usually have some kind of relationship. Aside from parent-subsidiary relationships, the arm's-length arrangement could be
in the form of export/import agent or distributorship.
Depending upon the nature of the licensed technology,
frequency of communication (daily, weekly, monthly, year-
ly) varies. In many cases, more frequent communication
and the parties' closeness have been identified as the main
factors behind the success of licensing arrangements.[15]

The Licensing Agreement

The licensing agreement is the written contract between the
licensor and the licensee. It specifies the rights and
obligations of each party. Each license agreement usually
states the type of licensing agreement, the licensed technology, the licensing restrictions, the obligations of each
party, and the compensation arrangements.

The agreement declares what will be transferred as a
result of the contract. It may be for patent rights only,
or for patent rights plus know-how. Typically, the contract is for both the patent rights and technical assistance
by the licensor (as a package or under separate contracts).
The license agreement may be for current know-how (technology) and only for one time, or for current plus future
developments and on a continuous basis.

The licensing agreement may contain sublicensing rights
and grant-back arrangements. A sublicensing right specifies the right of the licensee to transfer or reveal the
licensed technology to a third party. Grant-back arrangements deal with the transfer of improvements on the licensed technology from the licensee to the licensor.

The restrictions in the agreement may cover geographical limits, procurement, field of use, cross-licensing,
quality control, and modifications demanded by the licensee.
The agreement also includes compensation arrangements,
and legal and technical factors discussed earlier in this
chapter.

Licensing Impacts

The licensing arrangements have different impacts in the
source country (licensor's) and the recipient country (licensee's). This study focuses on the impacts of licensing
in the licensee's country. These impacts include, but are

not limited to, the following: (a) employment impacts—the licensed technology will have impacts on low-skilled, high-skilled, and managerial jobs in the licensee's market; (b) balance of payments impacts—the licensed technology (product or process) has a direct bearing on exports and imports of a country, the licensed technology typically substituting for similar imported products (though it could have export potential); (c) societal impacts—the licensed technology will use domestic goods (raw materials and products), and the licensing arrangements may have positive impacts on the quality of the environment, transportation and communication systems, and workers' health and safety; (d) income impacts—the positive result of the above is additional income not only to those directly involved but also to the government and the community.

REVERSE LICENSING
AND REVERSE INVESTMENT

International licensing of technology is an agreement whereby the owner of a technology (licensor) in one country licenses a foreign firm (licensee) to make use of the technology for (a) specified purpose(s) at an agreed fee. Reverse licensing occurs when the licensor is a foreign firm and the licensee is a U.S. firm.

FDI in the United States has been increasing rapidly since the early-to-mid-1970s. Most states have encouraged FDI (reverse investment or inward investment, as some states call it) by creating foreign investment promotion offices. Tax concessions, leased factories, and low-interest loans are among the incentives used to entice FDI. The major rationale for this activity is that it creates jobs and costs less than benefit payments to workers who would otherwise be unemployed.

The negative aspects of these foreign investment promotion activities are (1) the states forego tax dollars; (2) there is beginning to be some political backlash against foreign investment; (3) the concessions to the foreign investors can be interpreted as creating unfair competition for existing firms in the same industry.

It should also be noted that the foreign firms that invest in the United States tend to be MNCs, and they are relatively few in number. Consequently, most states are chasing after a relatively small number of firms, which are somewhat reluctant to invest fairly large sums under conditions of significant risk.

Reverse Licensing Instead of Reverse Investment

There are many small and medium-sized firms abroad that would like to get into the U.S. market place. Because they lack required (financial and marketing) resources, and because of the risks involved, they cannot invest directly in the United States. But they have other options: (1) they can set up their own sales offices and try to crack the U.S. market by exporting to it, but this is too expensive and risky for most of them; (2) they can find an import agent to handle their products for the U.S. market, but this is usually not effective; (3) they can license a U.S. company to produce the product in the United States and market the product, using the U.S. firm's marketing channels. This last strategy is usually the most attractive to the small and medium-sized foreign firms in terms of cost, risk, and effectiveness.

Why Don't More of These Firms
Look for U.S. Licensees?

Most of them don't even think of the idea. The few that do, have no mechanism to search for a U.S. partner. Why don't U.S. companies actively seek foreign licensors?
    Large U.S. MNCs have been doing this for years. They engage in two-way licensing and are actively scanning foreign countries on a continuing basis for new patents for which they might obtain a license in the U.S. market, where the product fits their product line. But the tens of thousands of smaller and medium-sized U.S. firms never consider this as a strategy, and would not know how to go about seeking an appropriate foreign licensor.

REVERSE LICENSING BENEFITS

Small and Medium-sized U.S. Firms

Most of these firms are one- or several-product companies that spend little or nothing on R&D. Without new and competitive technology, they go bankrupt as their product(s) reach(es) the end of the PLC. Reverse licensing is a new lease on life for these firms, permitting an expansion without any R&D expenditure. Last but not least, the costs of royalty payments are related directly to sales and/or profits of the licensee.

Small and Medium-sized Foreign Firms

Thousands of small and medium-sized firms in foreign countries that have the technology would like to enter the U.S. market. However, because of what was discussed earlier and a lack of financial and marketing resources, they cannot reach the U.S. market. There is no mechanism to provide them with the means of doing so. Reverse licensing will provide them with the mechanism and opportunities not possible otherwise.

Public Sector

How should state governments view reverse licensing?

1. Since reverse licensing is not as visible as FDI, it has no negative political repercussions.
2. It does not necessitate the granting of tax concessions and other costs by public authorities.
3. It can create as many jobs as does reverse investment, and does so more rapidly.
4. It is politically attractive because it assists many smaller and medium-sized domestic companies and creates jobs in many localities.
5. It is much easier and less costly to promote reverse licensing than reverse investment because the number of potential foreign licensors is very large, and they can make a positive decision more quickly because their costs and risks are much smaller than is true for the large, direct investment.

SUMMARY

As was stated and discussed in the section on the problem germane to this research in Chapter 1, there is an apparent need for a mechanism to match two groups of firms. The first group consists of tens of thousands of small and medium-sized U.S. firms that need new and competitive technology to survive. The second group consists of a fairly large number of small-to-medium-sized foreign firms. These firms have the technology needed in the United States, but because of huge capital and other required resources, they cannot directly invest in the United States. It was shown that licensing their technology to U.S. firms is a preferred strategy.

The mechanism for matching these two groups of firms

is reverse licensing, which will provide foreign firms having abundant supplies of technology with opportunities to license their technology and reach the U.S. market. Without reaching the U.S. market, many of these firms cannot prosper or even survive. Reverse licensing will extend their lives.

On the other hand, reverse licensing will provide tens of thousands of small-to-medium-sized U.S. firms with opportunities to get new and competitive technology. Without such technology (at a very competitive price, because of competition among overseas licensors), most of these firms cannot survive. Reverse licensing will be their savior by providing them with new or extended lives. In short, reverse licensing is an equilibrating mechanism that will match the supply of technology with the demand for that technology.

Before investigating reverse licensing in more detail and developing the research model, the related literature needs to be surveyed to see what others have to say about international licensing. Therefore, Chapter 4 will review the literature in order to provide the researcher with more insight on the subject. This will enable the researcher to draw on the previous discussions and the related literature, and build a model for attacking the problem.

4

Literature Review of International Technology Licensing

Concern over the implications of the international transfer of technology has heightened in the United States. Scholars, practitioners, congressional committees, and private and governmental institutions have focused on technology transfer and related issues. To date, all research on technology transfer has focused on the implications of such transfers from the United States and has taken a licensor's point of view. In this chapter licensing literature will be reviewed; in Chapter 5 the author will take a licensee's standpoint, and build on the preceding concepts, synthesize, introduce the research model, and propose the research hypotheses.

TECHNOLOGY LICENSING COMPENSATION

Farok J. Contractor has pursued the subject of technology transfer extensively. Most of his works have focused on the pricing, compensation, profitability, and policy implications of licensing from the licensor's viewpoint.[1]

Root and Contractor, using a sample of 102 recent licensing agreements in 41 countries made by 39 U.S. firms with independent licensees, developed a normative model of international licensing. Actual behavior of managers is compared with the normative model.

> In the normative model, both licensor and licensee have floor and ceiling prices determined by a number of factors; the final negotiated price is a point within the overlap between the 2 bid ranges,

or the bargaining range. The managers in the sample companies ranked factors considered in negotiating agreements, and regression analysis was used to identify variables systematically influencing compensation. Results indicate that actual negotiation differs from the model in two major respects:

1. The practice of satisficing rather than maximizing behavior on the part of licensors, and,
2. The lack of any explicit or systematic attention to opportunity costs.[2]

Perlitz investigated the compensation arrangements in international licensing and their impacts on market penetration, pricing policy, and conflicts between licensee and licensor:

It is worthwhile to study the impact of different compensatory arrangements in international licensing agreements on the market penetration abroad and to illustrate that particular forms of compensation may bring conflicts between the licensor and the licensee. Studies reveal that in practice the most commonly used forms of payment are based on lump sums and royalties paid either as a percentage of turnover or on the basis of dollar per unit. Royalties paid as a percentage of gross margin or as a percentage of profit before or after tax can hardly be found. Conflict may occur if the licensor wants to include a minimum sales volume in the agreement, the legality of this is questioned. American, German and European Community antitrust laws generally permit restrictions on the sales volume by the licensor. Only in the situation where these restrictions are part of a general system of restriction of competition are they against antitrust regulations. Finally, the licensor could also restrict the pricing decision of the licensee.[3]

Brecher[4] extended the theory of international trade in order to analyze the optimal commercial policy of a country importing technology for which royalties must be paid to foreigners. A basic model was developed that distinguishes between national and aggregate income, which differ by the royalties paid. Policy combinations for maximizing national welfare were derived, and the national gain or loss from introducing trade of technology was assessed. The analysis showed that maximization of national income can be achieved

if the home country combines a trade tax with a domestic
commodity-market tax or subsidy depending, respectively,
on whether the foreign country is a net exporter or importer of the commodity whose technology is licensed internationally. It was also demonstrated that the maximum level
of national welfare for the home country might be lower
with than without imported technology, if the foreign country exports the technology used to produce the commodity
exported by the home country.

Orleans (1982) in a mathematical model for pricing of
technology licensing argued that the licensing market bears
little resemblance to other markets, and it would be sur-
prising if the concept of a license price could be properly
examined in the context of conventional price theory. The
utility of a particular license will depend upon the level of
production set by a licensee, which in turn may depend not
only upon the licensee's cost schedule but also upon the
way in which the license price is formulated. Therefore,
net profit to the licensee will be revenue - cost - license
price.

> The profit as such represents a producer's surplus
> *not* a consumer's surplus and the producer's sur-
> plus is achieved without imposing any new cost on
> consumers. The profit from the licensed production
> represents a net addition to the wealth of the
> economy as a whole.

In general, the licensor's minimum price and the licensee's maximum price will be different. If both parties are
profit maximizers, neither will wish to concede to the other
more than necessary. The negotiated price should lie in a
permissible range that both parties can agree on. Otherwise no licensing agreement can take place.

> In a strictly two party system, the transaction
> price being apparently indeterminate [sic]. In this
> situation the licensor is faced with a monopolistic
> situation and must make the best of it. The situa-
> tion is entirely changed if there is more than one
> potential licensee who is competing in the same
> market. Suppose the licensor's minimum price in a
> two-party system is P_0 where $P_0 = R_1 - C_1$ or
> $P_0 = R_2 - C_2$ where R and C are the revenues and
> costs of the competing licenses with different pro-
> duction schedules. In this situation, it will be
> more profitable for the licensor to grant a license
> than not to do so. In general, the natural price of

an exclusive license will be the limiting price of the second highest bidder, the license going to the highest bidder at that price, $R_1 - C_1$.

Finnegan and Mintz take a practitioner point of view with regard to the methods of arriving at initial royalty figures for negotiating purposes. These techniques are the following:[5]

a. Viewing the royalty as the minimum return that the licensor reasonably expects to realize
b. Relating the royalty to be next best alternative available to the licensee
c. Considering the royalty in reference to royalty rates previously established by the licensor in similar agreements
d. Evaluating the royalty with reference to rates prevalent in the industry
e. Treating the royalty as a direct function of the forecasted profits or savings the licensee will derive from the exploitation of the licensed technology.

Method (a) produces the minimum royalty the licensor would accept, while method (b) provides the maximum royalty to which a licensee would reasonably agree. The figures produced by methods (c), (d), and (e) should provide additional points within the range defined by the figures produced by (a) and (b). By using as many of the five methods as are readily adaptable to the given situation, the licensing parties can effectively determine the range of possible royalties and focus on that range during negotiations.

PROFITABILITY OF TECHNOLOGY LICENSING

Branson focused on the accounting measurement of profitability of licensing.[6] Caves et al. and Rodriguez focused on the costs of technology transfer.[7] Behrman and Schmidt, through a normative behavioral model, show the negotiating behavior of the licensor and licensee executives.[8]

Contractor, in a study of U.S. firms' licensing practices, showed that the increasing importance and incidence of licensing for U.S. firms, and the concomitant regulatory and legal changes concerning patents and trademarks, have created concern about a weakening patent system and technology losses.[9] His conclusion, in a study of 241 U.S.

firms involved in technology licensing, revealed that there is little threat of losing technology. Regression results showed that small and medium-sized firms were more active in licensing agreements than was previously thought. The size of the firm was the most important factor in the number of licensing agreements undertaken. Larger, international companies did more licensing. Strategy motivations for licensing included lump-sum fees, royalties, new market entry, and other short-term income-generating strategies. The incidence of patents and trademarks was highest in the chemical, pharmaceutical, petroleum, and food processing industries. Thus, a weakening trademark system would hurt those industries most.

Mansfield, Romeo, and Wagner investigated the effect of American foreign trade on R&D activity. The sample chosen was broken into two subsamples: 20 firms in the fabricated metal products, machinery, instruments, textile, paper, and tire industries; and 10 major chemical companies. Both subsamples evidenced interfirm variation that may reflect differences in the percentage of sales abroad and the amount of R&D spending. The regression results indicated that development projects have a smaller share of their returns from abroad than do research projects. The firms were asked to estimate the effect on R&D if they could not use new technology abroad, or could not export products or processes based on the technology. The firms indicated that expenditures would fall.

> When industry is held constant, there is no significant relationship between a firm's foreign sales and the ratio of R&D spending to sales. Firms with high foreign sales are more concerned with basic research and long term projects. Product innovations are more likely to be transferred abroad than process innovations, and foreign subsidiaries are the most frequently used channels of international technology transfer.[10]

Teece found that transfer costs were higher when underlying technology was labor-intensive (disembodied) than when it was capital-intensive (embodied). Presumably, the former involves a much greater need for specially skilled resources in facilitating transfer, whereas capital-intensive technology is principally "embodied" in new machinery or equipment, and therefore is simpler to communicate and transfer.[11]

MOTIVATIONS OF TECHNOLOGY LICENSING
AND CONFLICTS OF INTEREST

Millman, in analyzing MNCs' technology transfer incentives and intergovernmental conflicts affecting the transfer, concluded that:

The impetus behind technology is two-fold:

1. The desire of multinational corporations (MNC) to control and manage their technologies in worldwide markets, and
2. The benefits to be gained by sharing technology.

MNCs undoubtedly will remain the primary channel for technology transfer in private sector unless other efficient channels are developed. Licensing is a widespread practice among MNCs to extend ownership, and it contributes greatly to the complexity of technology transfer. Although Third World nations and newly developing countries are exerting pressure for more equitable technology transfer, they have gained little access to needed forms of basic technology. Governments view technology transfer as part of the foreign policy arena; thus, governments can have significant impact on promoting or hindering the transfer process. Particular examples of intergovernmental conflicts affecting technology transfer include:

1. US/USSR/Western Europe disagreements following the invasion of Afghanistan,
2. Brazil's nationalistic attitude toward imported technology, and
3. The Peoples Republic of China's first steps into international markets.[12]

Millman focused on international technology licensing and investigated the factors contributing to the success or failure of licensing contracts. He argued that the transfer of technology through licensing is controversial. A licensor receives financial benefits and profits from broader markets, but some firms are hesitant because of a potential lack of control over licensee operations.

Successful licensing requires an organizational environment inclined toward firm management commitment. A license package is a broad range of technical, organizational, and commercial knowledge that supports the transferred technology. License packages can include patents, trademarks, procedures, and sales support material. Confidentiality is difficult to ensure in licensing negotiations. Payments, which require careful negotiations, usually include a combination of a down payment, progress payments, and minimum and running royalties. Although some firms resent the dominant role of multinational corporations (MNCs) in licensing, small companies can benefit from the resources of the MNC. Negotiators should be aware of unwritten business rules and ethical standards of foreign countries. Most failures at licensing result from a breakdown of communications between the parties. [13]

TECHNOLOGY LICENSING AND ITS SPEED OF TRANSFER

Vernon and Davidson, in a study of 221 innovations by 32 U.S. MNEs, found that speed of transfer had become faster over time (1945–77). [14] They also found that the relative importance of licensing decreased (from 31.4 percent in 1945–55 to 19.8 percent in 1966–75), and MNCs increased the use of their subsidiaries (from 68.6 percent to 80.2 percent during that same period), for the transfer of technology rather than use independent licensees. [15] (See Table 4.1.)

Mansfield focused on speed of technology transfer, [16] and his findings were reinforced and supported by Benvignati of the Federal Trade Commission. Benvignati, in empirical research on 40 textile machinery innovations and their speed of transfer between U.S. and leading foreign competitors, concluded that:

> . . . the speed of international transfer has been greater as time has passed and as commercial transactions between industrialized nations have increased. The speed has been slower when the innovating domestic firm was technologically dominant. The data reveal that 88% of the licensed transfers and 100% of the FDI transfers involved technologically nondominant firms and imitators. Because advanced countries have roughly equivalent capacities to lend support to high technology activities and roughly comparable patterns of domestic

TABLE 4.1 Transfers of Innovations by MNE's to Foreign Manufacturing Subsidiaries and Independent Licensees, by Period of U.S. Introduction

Period of U.S. Introduction	Same Year or 1 Year After	2 or 3 Years After	4 or 5 Years After	6 to 9 Years After	10 or More Years After	Total
1945-55 (94 innovations)						
Via subsidiaries	14	18	11	43	233	319
Via licensees	1	9	28	16	92	146
Subsidiaries as % of total	93.3	66.7	28.2	72.9	71.7	68.6
1956-65 (70 innovations)						
Via subsidiaries	24	39	21	46	49	179
Via licensees	7	10	15	13	22	67
Subsidiaries as % of total	77.4	79.6	58.3	78.0	69.0	72.8
1966-75 (57 innovations)						
Via subsidiaries	22	37	21	16	1	97
Via licensees	2	4	10	6	2	24
Subsidiaries as % of total	97.7	90.2	67.7	72.7	33.3	80.2
Total, 1945-75						
Via subsidiaries	60	94	53	105	283	595
Via licensees	10	23	53	35	116	237
Subsidiaries as % of total	85.7	80.3	50.0	75.0	70.9	71.5

Source: R. Vernon and Davidson, W., "The Speed of Technology Transfer by U.S. MNCs to Overseas Subsidiaries and Independent Licensees" (1979), p. 63.

needs and preferences, the speed with which new technologies spread across such countries is not usually thought to be constrained by national levels of R&D infrastructure and scientific capabilities or by lags in domestic demands. Communication and competitive variables which may vary across industries or across specific innovations within an industry are potentially more important determinants than country differences.[17]

TECHNOLOGY LICENSING AND DEPENDENCE ISSUE

Lake found that almost all British licensees in the semiconductor industry were dependent on their U.S. licensors.[18] He also found that the diffusion lag (time elapsed between U.S. introduction and utilization by the British licensees) was more than three years.

John P. Killing has done the most comprehensive study of manufacturing under license in Canada.[19] Examining only Canadian-owned firms in the secondary manufacturing sector, he found that firms with strong R&D capabilities often obtained licenses early in their life cycle and faced no export restrictions. His conclusion was that although manufacturing under license provides a continuous flow of technology to firms with no R&D capability, it is not a good strategy for long-term growth, the reason being an unhealthy degree of dependence upon the licensor. He argued that licensing of this type is beneficial only to firms that are using it as a means to an end, that end being the establishment of an in-house R&D competence.

Killing also discussed licensing and the formation of joint ventures from the perspective of the technologically dependent firm.[20] The conditions under which a firm without technology should attempt to acquire it, via either of two kinds of license agreement and two kinds of joint venture, were also addressed. Examination of data on 74 license agreements and 28 joint ventures indicated that the market for technology is fragmented and inconsistent. A normative model was described; it suggested the conditions under which technology-deficient firms should and should not make use of current technology license agreements, future technology license agreements, joint ventures in which they own a strong controlling interest, and joint ventures in which they are roughly or exactly equal owners with the technology supplier. Under some conditions, buying technology is not a viable corporate strategy, but it can be effective under certain circumstances.

Wills, in a sample of 283 of the most profitable products and manufacturing processes introduced by Canadian firms, concluded that "Licensing was not found to be a significant means of obtaining technology."[21] Crookell argued that the technology transfer process was more efficient within the firm (parent-subsidiary) than between unaffiliated firms.[22]

VIABILITY OF TECHNOLOGY LICENSING AS AN INTERNATIONALIZATION STRATEGY

Zenoff concluded that "foreign licensing has not been used as a deliberate marketing device and appears to be a residual type of activity." Tesar, in an empirical study of medium-sized U.S. firms, found that "the majority of firms do not consider licensing as a viable alternative."[23]

Carstairs and Welch, in a study of Australian firms, concluded that:

> The mainly small to medium-sized companies in our investigation tend to utilize licensing because of various constraints on the use of other international marketing techniques, rather than because of a positive preference for licensing as such. Despite its adoption in a secondary or residual manner . . . many firms were still able to successfully expand their international operations via licensing. A key factor in the success of licensing appeared to be the development of effective interaction with licensee in a long term relationship.[24]

Ford and Ryan focused on the importance of the marketing of technology in improving the return on investment by technology source firms.[25] Companies facing high R&D costs, competitive pressures, capacity limitations, financial difficulties, antitrust laws, and foreign trade barriers must improve the rate of return on technology investments by marketing technology during all phases of its life cycle. The technology life cycle (TLC), which pinpoints the changing decisions companies face, has the following states:

1. Technology development
2. Technology application
3. Application launch
4. Application growth
5. Technology maturity
6. Degraded technolgoy

Complete marketing of a technology requires the following:

1. Development of a coherent strategy for a full portfolio of technologies
2. Decisions on acquisition or devestment of technologies
3. Awareness of the value of developing technology for direct sales
4. A clear understanding of the relationship between the sale of technology through licensing and the sale of products based on that technology
5. Recognition of the technology buyer's knowledge of its needs
6. Reliance on technology marketers.[26]

Caves, Crookell, and Killing examined "market imperfections in licensing of technology" and concluded that:

Licensing agreements result from a basis on costs and uncertainties of contractual agreements between opportunistic parties. Surveys are conducted of licensors and licensees, concentrating on two classes of hypotheses about imperfections in the market:

1. Licensees take part in a market for specific advantage.
2. Each license agreement is viewed as a Pareto-optimal.[27]

Analysis indicated that license agreements fail to capture the full rent for the licensor, thereby enabling the licensee to emerge from the transaction in a stronger position. Technological licenses are becoming more important in international commerce. Generally, both the source and the recipient countries lose if technology transfers that otherwise would have occurred through joint ownership are diverted and no transfer agreements have taken place.

Finan examined licensing in Britain's semiconductor industry from U.S. licensors' viewpoint.[28] He found that U.S. licensors didn't consider licensing as a major means of technology transfer, and basically granted patent licenses as well as technological assistance. Large U.S. firms, such as Western Electric, Texas Instruments, and Fairchild, intended to be licensors, and the royalties charged by them were found to be a function of

1. The number of licenses covering the agreement
2. The technological capabilities of licensees—firms with strong R&D capabilities often receive royalty-free

licenses and the licensor gets to use the new developments of the licensed technology via grant-backs
3. The licensor's licensing competition.

The Industrial Research Institute, in its position statement on licensing of technology, concluded that transferring
of technology between countries or corporations, and from
universities and private individuals to commercial enterprises, is affected by the licensing of patents and
know-how. The government influences this flow of technology through patent laws, antitrust actions, research by
government employees, and government-funded research in
universities and contract laboratories.

In order to promote technology transfer, private-
ly-owned patents should not be subject to compulso-
ry licensing. The government should grant exclusive licenses to government-owned patents, and the
no-royalty, no-fee basis for the granting of nonexclusive licenses to government should be discon-
tinued. Innovative efforts of private inventors
should be supported, and the inventions originating
at the university level should remain the property
of the university. These recommendations are
based on the studies made by the Industrial Research Institute in 1978.[29]

The U.S. Department of Commerce takes a licensor's
viewpoint, with the presumption that any time a U.S.
company is involved in a transfer of technology (a licensing
agreement or FDI) the transferor (licensor) is always a
U.S. company and the recipient (licensee) is always a
non-U.S. firm. The following is a checklist provided by
the Department of Commerce to potential U.S. licensors and
foreign direct investors:[30]

1. If processes are involved, spell out the areas of appli-
    cation and use by the licensee, and establish control
    and periodic review of the licensee's operations.
2. It is important to provide for conditions under which
    the licensee may or may not manufacture competing or
    noncompeting products.
3. Establish the right to institute and enforce a standard
    of quality with particular relation to the use of your
    trademarks, where permitted.
4. Establish the right to inspect the licensee's operations,
    to receive and evaluate samples of products, to audit
    books, and to survey licensee sales and advertising

efforts at stated intervals.
5. It is desirable to train the licensee's personnel in advance of and during the licensed operations; consider where and when to train, how many trainees at a time, and for how long. (Establish a basis for payment of training costs and distinguish these costs from royalty obligations.)
6. There should be provisions for special research and engineering on behalf of the licensee. (Clearly define the scope and time, and assess the costs against the licensee on a cost basis.)
7. Provide for the handling of future disputes with the licensee.
8. Reserve the right to modify or terminate the license if unsatisfactory changes occur in the ownership or key personnel of the licensee.
9. Define the rights and obligations of both parties after termination, including the effect of waivers.

Ruzic focused on the technology transfer between the National Aeronautics and Space Administration (NASA) and industries, and argued that the most effective pacesetter in technology has been the space program.[31] NASA's technology transfer arm—the Technology Utilization Branch—uses a person-to-person approach to exchange its information with industry. NASA has established a network of industrial applications centers. The centers, located at six universities, provide technical assistance and literature retrieval. The network is the largest information storehouse in the world. The centers interact with NASA field centers. Another method of transferring technology is the biomedical and technology applications teams. These teams try to apply NASA technology to problems encountered in medical facilities and public sector agencies. NASA maintains a patent licensing program.

Stuart investigated technology transfer, patents, and licensing, and concluded that the patent system creates property out of new technology.[32] Patents must be obtained in every country where protection is required. They are obtained in different countries in order to

1. Provide exclusive future protection
2. Defend freedom of action
3. Provide licensing for income
4. Provide licensing for information.

Companies that have in-house patents can negotiate licensing agreements more easily because the licensing company feels that the licensee has prior valuable experience. Licensees must know what is wanted in the agreement and what can be paid for it. A company without technical know-how needs more than a simple patent agreement. While licensing can reduce the risk of new product innovation, there must be in-house R&D to maintain a level of technical competence.

TECHNOLOGY LICENSING AND INTERNATIONAL COOPERATION

Hill studied international industrial marketing in the Eastern bloc countries and the advantages to Western firms.[33] He found that since the late 1960s, the number of industrial cooperation agreements between Western companies and eastern European foreign trade organizations had increased substantially. In a sample of industrial cooperation agreements, it was found that there were three major types of these agreements:

1. Coproduction based on the specialization of partners
2. The supply of licenses, with payments in products manufactured under the licenses
3. The supply of plant and equipment, with payment in resultant products manufactured by the plant supplied.

Hill argued that there are advantages to Western firms in East-West industrial cooperation, such as gaining access to new markets and profitability. However, there are disadvantages as well, including high initial marketing costs. An examination of six case studies of British engineering companies engaged in industrial cooperation with eastern European foreign trade organizations indicated that such agreements are complex in terms of design, development, production, costing, and finance. The British companies were able to secure advantages, but not without some difficulty.

Kiser focused on East-West technology transfer and how U.S. firms can acquire Eastern bloc technology.[34]

The Council for Mutual Economic Assistance (COMECON) develops many innovations that U.S. companies would find useful if they knew about them and how to get them. U.S.-COMECON commercial contact is very low, however. U.S. companies that buy such technology do so mainly because it represents a better or cheaper way to do something. They can buy a license in which one party grants certain use rights and/or know-how to another.

COMECON has sold only about 1,500 licenses to market economy nations since 1965. Its poor performance in selling licenses is due primarily to lack of commercial contact. Personal contact is crucial, since many COMECON technologies are in the R&D stage or are process technology: "Successful licensing with COMECON requires honesty, good communications, mutual respect, and especially good personal relationships."[35] The licensee should be able to make crucial technical improvements. It is also necessary that contracts be detailed and carefully written.

Business Week investigated the process of tapping Soviet bloc technology by U.S. firms and found that products and processes licensed from Eastern bloc countries represent a small but growing flow of technology.[36] International trade experts believe much technology remains to be discovered, since 30 percent of the world's patents are held by citizens or organizations within the Soviet sphere of influence. According to John W. Kiser III, the nearly 50 identified licenses from Soviet bloc countries are only the beginning of exploitable technology (see Table 2.9). New drugs are routinely sought among the eastern European countries; two new anti-cancer drugs have recently been developed in the USSR. Soft contact lenses are the result of Czechoslovakian research. A new surgical stapler to close incisions faster is a Soviet development. The Soviet bloc countries are very strong in basic academic research, while the United States is very strong in applied research.

U.S. corporations have utilized the Soviet technology, and since the mid-1960s the technology purchased from the Soviets has started to yield military applications.[37]

The voice of the LDCs as the recipients of technology from the developed nations is usually echoed through international institutions and conferences such as the U.N. Conference on Trade and Development (UNCTAD), the U.N. Industrial Development Organization, (UNIDO), and the World Intellectual Property Organization (WIPO). Their major arguments have focused on the pricing and appropriateness of technology. These organizations argue that technology is a public good and should be transferred to LDCs at no or very low cost.

The transferred technology is not appropriate for most recipient LDCs because the technolgoy developed in the industrialized countries is usually capital-intensive and LDCs need labor-intensive technology. Most LDCs are overpopulated and need technology that will provide employment for their residents. Cultural differences associated with technology transfer and the resultant problems are beyond the scope of this study.

Committees have been formed with the aim of introducing a new code of conduct for the international transfer of technology. Recent UNCTAD and WIPO meetings have resolved that such a code be introduced by the United Nations. Developed nations, having a great interest and a great deal at stake, cannot afford to ignore such meetings, and have actively participated in the formulation of the new code of conduct.

Joelson focused on U.S. laws and the proposed code of conduct governing the transfer of technology. He argued that developing nations assert that:

> Technology is the universal heritage of mankind and . . . legally binding rules must be adopted to shield their economies and nations from undesirable licensing practices by transnational enterprises who control the bulk of technology. Developed nations feel guidelines should be voluntary and that freedom of contract should continue in this area.[38]

Almost all of the above works have looked at international technology licensing from the U.S. licensors' standpoint. There are good reasons for the existence of such a bias. For decades, U.S. corporations had the leading role in FDI and licensing their technology to foreign licensees. Recently, the trend has been reversed and foreign firms have been exploiting the U.S. market by means of various strategies: export, FDI, licensing, and/or a combination of all three.

This book reverses what has been discussed so far and conceptualizes it into a research model and research hypotheses. In Chapter 5, the focus will be on international technology licensing from the licensees' standpoint, and the research model as well as the research hypotheses will be introduced. A model for evaluating various options open to a firm in need of technology will also be presented.

5

The Research Model
and the
Research Hypotheses

THE RESEARCH MODEL

This chapter synthesizes the preceding discussions by bringing together concepts and variables related to technology licensing. Pieces are put together to build the research model with a focus on technology licensing from a licensee's standpoint. This chapter consists of two main parts. In the first, concepts are synthesized and the research model is developed; in the second, the research hypotheses are proposed.

In developing the model, the main focus is on two things: (1) the licensee's characteristics, such as the firm's size, technical and marketing competence, and dominance (compared with the licensor); and (2) the types of license agreement (one-time vs. continuous), which were discussed in Chapter 3.

The main logic for focusing on the licensee's characteristics and the type of license agreement is to find out the conditions under which firms manufacture under license, their motivations, and the relationship between licensees' characteristics and the type of license agreement to which they commit themselves.

In building the research model, the focus is on "horizontal" technology transfer (between two firms) on an arms' length basis. In Chapter 3, it was argued that this type of technology transfer is the classical one, and most of the licensing agreements that take place are between two unaffiliated firms. The licensors do not want (or cannot afford) to commit a large amount of capital, and the political risks are the least for them. The licensees' motivations are, essentially, related to costs, risks, and time. They enter the agreement because the costs and the risks are lower, or the licensed product(s) could reach the market faster.

The licensees' characteristics determine their motivations and the type of license agreement. As was stated in Chapter 3, technology transfer does not occur at the science level, because there is nothing concrete to license. Therefore, the transfer is limited to (or takes place at) the technology or production level.

Licensees with core skills can enter licensing agreements at both levels; licensees without core skills are limited to the production level. At this level, though, the licensee needs to have at least some engineering knowledge for the transfer to take place. Thus, licensees are not homogeneous or identical, and the level at which they acquire technology is a function of their core skills. The type of agreement entered is also a function of the licensees' core skills and of the type of technology involved (industry-specific).

In Chapter 3 it was stated that every year thousands of small-to-medium-sized firms are forced into bankruptcy because they are one- or few-product firms. Once their product(s) reach the end of the life cycle, they must either develop or acquire new and competitive technology, or cease operations. The new technology has to be developed internally (most small-to-medium-sized firms lack the required resources) or to be acquired externally (through licensing). The possibility of taking a license from another U.S. firm is remote, for the obvious reason that no U.S. firm would like to create competition for itself in the domestic market.

In developing strategies for future technological needs, a firm needs to evaluate its own characteristics prior to choosing a strategy. Figure 5.1 summarizes the options available to a firm in need of technology and shows where licensing fits in (as a licensee).

Prior to introducing the LCM, it is appropriate to introduce a valuation model as a framework for analyzing options open to the licensee. Essentially, decisions related to taking a license are long-term in nature and have a major impact on the success or failure of the firm. Therefore, the firm (licensee) must carefully evaluate the various options prior to commiting itself to a particular strategy (see Figures 5.1 and 5.3).

Figure 5.1 Developing Strategies for Future Technological Needs: Where Licensing Fits In, from Licensee's Standpoint

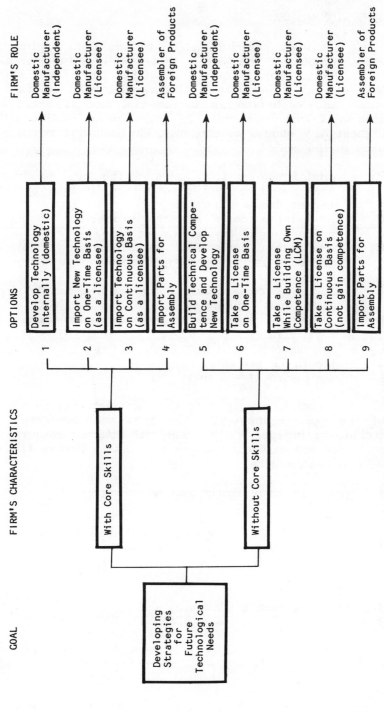

Source: Based on original material compiled by the author.

THE NPV MODEL

Firms use various techniques in making their capital budgeting decisions. The NPV is theoretically a superior method in corporate capital budgeting. The firm should find the NPV of each alternative by incorporating all relevant revenues and costs (on an incremental and after-tax basis) associated with each option. Then the alternative with the highest NPV should be chosen. The following notations are used in the model:

R_t = total revenues from sales of the final product that uses the firm-specific advantage (technology)—firm's own or licensed technology

C_t = total input costs for the production of the final product using firm's own technology

C_t^* = total input costs for the production of the final product using licensing arrangement (firm is a licensee)

A_t^* = additional costs incurred by the firm for development of the new technology

L_t^* = additional costs due to licensing fees (lump-sum or royalty rate)

d_i = the discount rate (i = 1, 2, 3 $\cdots$)

T = the firm's tax rate

t = time period (t = 0 to t = N)

Two options are open to the manufacturing firm in need of the new technology. The firm can develop its own technology independently, using its internal resources (I), or it can use external sources and take a license (L). The NPV of each will be:

(1) development of firm's own technology

$$\text{NPV}_I = \sum_{t=0}^{N} \frac{(R_t - C_t - A_t^*)(1-T)}{(1 + d_1)} \quad (1)$$

(2) taking a license (licensee)

$$\text{NPV}_L = \sum_{t=0}^{N} \frac{(R_t - C_t^* - L_t^*)(1-T)}{(1 + d_2)} \quad (2)$$

The return/risk trade-offs are assumed to be different because of different risks, cash flow patterns, and timing for each alternative. Also, the licensing fees are in dollars (L_t*). If the fees are percentages (percent of sales or revenues), the dollar amount should be found or the revenues should be adjusted for the royalty payments. Also, all the cash flows are assumed to be known with certainty. If the cash flows are not known with certainty, the certainty equivalent or risk-adjusted technique could be used. By calculating the NPV of each alternative, the alternative with higher NPV will be found and preferred. If the NPVs for both alternatives are negative (NPV<0), neither alternative will be chosen. The firm may be better off if it becomes a distributor (assembler) instead of a manufacturer when the NPV of importing (NPV_D) is positive and the highest among the alternatives. This case is not central to this study because the focus is on the manufacturing firms. Therefore:

1. Develop own technology when

$$NPV_I > max\ (NPV_L, NPV_D) \qquad (3)$$

2. Take a license (as a licensee) when

$$NPV_L > max\ (NPV_I, NPV_D) \qquad (4)$$

3. Become an importer (assembler-distributor) when

$$NPV_D > max\ (NPV_L, NPV_I) \qquad (5)$$

Since the focus is on manufacturing with and without license, the first two alternatives will be of interest and will be analyzed.

Obviously, these two alternatives do not have the same characteristics. First, the risks associated with the first option are far higher than those associated with the latter because of the uncertainties involved in investing in R&D and the probability of failure. It is quite possible that the amounts invested in core skills do not produce new technology. Such is not the case when the firm acquires the technology through licensing arrangements. The licensor has already developed the technology and has patented it, so the risk of failure is extremely low or nonexistent.

Second, the cash-flow patterns are different for each alternative. The former requires substantially larger amounts of investment at the beginning of the project, because of the costs associated with the employment of core skills (far more than the down payment for licensing of technology). The cash flows throughout the life of the project are higher in the first case because there is no royalty payment (internalization).

Third, the timing of the cash flow and the introduction of the new product into the market are different for each alternative. In the first case, it might take years before the technology is developed, if it is every developed. This is not the case for the licensing alternative. The investment at the beginning is far less in that case, and in most instances the licensee can negotiate an agreement without any down payment. The royalty payments are also contingent on the success of the licensee. Thus, like any other problem of capital budgeting under risk (uncertainty), it is appropriate to use a certainty equivalent technique (coefficient = ≅) or risk-adjusted discount rate to adjust the cash flow or the discount rate associated with each option in proportion to the uncertainties of each alternative.

THE LCM

A licensee enters into a license agreement for various reasons. Generally, licensing of technology (from a licensee's viewpoint) is a long-term investment or capital budgeting decision. A licensee has two options prior to licensing of technology: (1) develop its own R&D capabilities and then develop new technology, or (2) acquire the technology through licensing. The cost of its own R&D, the probability of failure, the time involved, and the strong patent laws are the most important factors in favor of taking a license. The adaptation costs, the time needed for negotiation, the advantages of strengthening its own R&D, independence, and other considerations (such as the NIH syndrome) are among the most important factors against taking a license.

The LCM builds on Killing's licensing cycle and tries to show the validity of the model as an alternative growth strategy to the licensee's developing its own R&D and technology.

Based on LCM, the licensees with continuous licensing agreements have better chances of going through the licensing cycle than those with one-time agreements. In Figure 5.2, the process through which the licensee goes before achieving technical competence is explained.

Figure 5.2 Licensing Cycle Model

Stage 1:   The U.S. firm, with a low R&D competence in an industry where
           technical innovations are very important, is confronted with
           international competition.

Stage 2:   Because of its lack of R&D and new technology, the firm is
           unable to compete effectively. It enters a licensing agreement
           on a continuous basis with a foreign firm and starts production
           under license. The license usually is a complete technical
           assistance agreement.

Stage 3:   As the manufacturing starts and sales volume grows, the licensee
           begins to develop its own technical capacities with licensor's
           assistance. Gradually production difficulties decline, the
           licensee's R&D capabilities increase, and its dependence on the
           licensor is reduced.

Stage 4:   The licensee develops enough of an in-house R&D competence to
           cancel or renegotiate the license agreement. Stage 4 could come
           a long time (up to 10 years) after Stage 2.

Source: Based on J. Peter Killing's licensing model in
his "Manufacturing Under License in Canada" (Ph.D. diss.,
University of Western Ontario, 1975), p. 184.

STRATEGIC PLANNING

It is important to note that the licensee may or may not
have entered (or will enter) the licensing cycle without
prior planning. Some licensees do go through the stages of
LCM as part of their strategic planning. They have chosen
(or choose) to go the licensing route in order to build up
their technical competence.

The reasons behind such a decision are numerous.
Cost is perhaps the most important reason. As with capital
budgeting decisions, the licensee has two alternatives with
different return and risk trade-offs. The licensee using
the NPV approach has preferred the licensing alternative
over the development of in-house R&D. The costs associated with licensing are basically the adaptation costs and
the compensations to the licensor on an opportunity-cost
basis. The costs associated with the second alternative are
essentially those of hiring R&D personnel and developing
the new product.

A second reason is the risks involved in the development of new products. The probability of failure is much higher for a firm without R&D competence that decides to build its in-house R&D team and develop products than for a firm that chooses the licensing route. The reason is that the licensor has already developed the product and its future success is known with relative certainty. When a firm acquires the needed technology through continuous licensing arrangements, it has a better chance of building its own in-house R&D competence, and the technical and marketing risks are lower.

A third reason is timing. It could well be a number of years before the firm builds its own R&D competence and develops a new product—if it ever manages to develop and introduce the product. The risks are great for the small and medium-sized firms, and most cannot survive that long. Therefore, the firm has a much better chance of success with the licensing alternative. The product reaches the market faster and the licensee acquires the needed expertise throughout the process, with the licensor's assistance.

Finally, patent laws are very important in the choice for or against taking a license. If patent laws are strong and enforced in the licensor's, as well as the licensee's, market, the licensee cannot circumvent the patent.

A firm in need of technology has a total of nine options (see Figure 5.1). Options 1, 4, 5, and 9 are not central to this study, because the focus is on evaluating the viability of the licensing option from a licensee's standpoint. Thus, the discussion will be limited to five options and conditions under which each option is acceptable. Again, the type of licensing agreement and the type of licensed technology are dependent on the licensee's core skills. Figure 5.3 shows these five options from that standpoint.

Option 1

The licensee has technical capabilities and can take a license for technology, whether or not commercially proven: technology transfer can take place at the technology and production levels. The licensee that takes a license on a one-time basis does so because of the existence of a patent. Because of the licensee's competence, the expectations are that the technology transfer agreements could occur at both earlier and later stages of the PLC. In some cases, the licensee acquires the rights to the technology because taking a license is the least expensive option (U.S. versus overseas cost of R&D). Also because of the licensee's

Figure 5.3 Developing Strategies for Future Technological Needs: The Licensee's Options

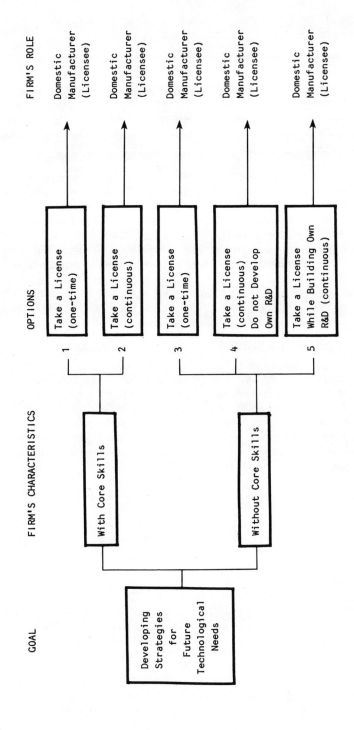

Source: Based on original material compiled by the author.

69

technical competence, taking a license will not make the licensee dependent on the licensor.

Option 2

This option is quite different from the first one. The licensee has the competence but acquires the technology through licensing on a continuous basis. Its motive is, essentially, cost-related. The licensee is expected to have cross-licensing arrangements with the licensor. The parties have more or less the same capabilities, and the licensing agreement is for mutal benefit. It is also possible that the licensor does not have the required resources (financial or marketing) to exploit the licensee's market on its own (through export or FDI). The technology transfer can take place at the technology and production levels. Taking a license is a capital budgeting decision. There are numerous examples of such licensing arrangements, including AT&T and Olivetti of Italy, AMC and Renault of France, Chrysler and Volkswagen of West Germany and Mitsubishi of Japan.

Option 3

The licensee does not have technical competence but buys technology on a one-time basis. The technology transfer can happen only at the production level because of the licensee's characteristics. Even at this level, the licensee must have some engineering competence for the adaptation of the technology. At the production level, the technology is commercially proven and the technology transfer takes place at the later stage of the PLC. The technological changes are not that frequent for the licensed technology.

Option 4

The licensee does not have the technical competence and acquires technology on a continuous basis. The technology should be commercially proven and the licensing takes place at the later stage of the PLC. The type of technology is expected to be non-R&D-intensive because (1) the licensee lacks technical competence, and (2) the chances are that the licensor would prefer to exploit the licensee's market on its own and internalize the advantages. In the long run, there might be an unhealthy dependence on the licensor. If the technology is available from various sources (competitive licensors' market) and the technology is not of strategic importance, then the chances of such a dependence are remote. In this case, licensing is an acceptable option.

Option 5

The licensee does not have the core skills, but licensing is considered the first step toward competence and is part of the licensee's strategic planning. The licensee acquires the technology and gradually builds its own in-house R&D. The type of technology involved will be commercially proven, and the licensing takes place at a later stage of the PLC. This is essentially the case with the LCM described in this chapter. If the licensee proceeds as planned and acquires the competence within the planned period, perhaps this alternative is the preferred strategy.

Prior to the introduction of the research variables and the hypotheses, it is appropriate to define and operationalize the variables used in the model:

A. Licensees' Characteristics

1. Firm Size

    a. Small—A licensee with fewer than 100 employees and/or less than $25 million in annual sales
    b. Medium—A licensee with 100–499 employees and/or $25–100 million in annual sales
    c. Large—A licensee with more than 500 employees and/or more than $100 million in annual sales

2. Core Skills

    a. A licensee is considered technically competent (with core skills) if it has more than 25 qualified scientists and engineers per 1,000 employees and/or spends more than 3.5 percent of its net sales on R&D activities
    b. A licensee that does not meet the above criterion is classified as a licensee without core skills

3. Dominance

    A dominant licensee is one that is larger than its licensor in terms of number of employees, sales, and/or R&D expenditures. Otherwise it is considered a nondominant licensee

B. Characteristics of Licensed Technology

1. Technical and Marketing Uncertainty

    a. Low—An example is the uncertainties associated with a standardized product (for instance, many home appliances)

    b. Medium—The technology changes relatively often in terms of input and the manufacturing process

    c. High—An example is a new product. The technology, the process, and the inputs change frequently. Growth industries are essentially of this type[1]

2. The PLC

The technology (product) is assumed to go through several stages[2] (see Chapter 3)

C. The Licensees' Motivations

Licensees' motivations were explained in Chapter 3. Briefly, they were related to cost, risk, time, or a combination of all three.

Licensees enter licensing agreements because the costs associated with licensing are lower than those of building their own R&D capabilities and developing new technology. The risks associated with licensing (from a licensee standpoint) are lower because of the probability of failure associated with in-house R&D. Timing is extremely important, having a direct bearing on the profitability and attractiveness of various projects. Licensing will enable the licensee to manufacture the product and get it to the market faster.

THE LICENSING AGREEMENT: TYPE AND RESTRICTIONS

Crookell classified licensing agreements into three major categories:[3]

1. All technology currently developed or to be developed by licensor

2. All technology now in place by the licensor (the licensee must have in-house skills to develop future changes)

3. License for a specified patented product, component, or process.

The first type includes future technology developed by the licensor and therefore is "continuous." The other types are basically "one-time." In this book the licensing agreement types are divided into two broad categories:

1. Continuous—A lasting but renewable agreement
2. One-time—This category includes a license for a patent only or for patent plus technical know-how (see Chapters 3 and 7 for detailed analysis).

The licensing restrictions are those explained in Chapter 3: geographical, procurement, and cross-licensing.

THE RESEARCH FOCUS

Since there are no previous studies on technology licensing from the U.S. licensees' standpoint, this study is unique. The research is exploratory in nature and unique in its hypotheses. It investigates the following issues from the U.S. licensees' standpoint:

1. The identification of the types of licensees in the United States (Ohio) and their characteristics, such as size and technical competence
2. The characteristics of the licensed technology, such as the stage of PLC and technical or marketing uncertainty
3. The licensees' characteristics (such as dominance and the pricing of the licensed technology (such as royalty rate), and the restrictions imposed by the licensor
4. The identification of the type of licensing agreement (one-time vs. continuous) and licensees' characteristics (such as technical competence)
5. The licensees' motivations for entering licensing agreements; the viability of licensing as a growth strategy
6. The licensing impact as viewed by U.S. licensees.

On the basis of the above issues and the previous discussions, the research hypotheses will be formulated.

THE RESEARCH HYPOTHESES

The first six hypotheses deal with the effects of the licensees' characteristics (size, technical competence, and so on). The last two focus on the type of license agreement (one-time or continuous). These hypotheses are explained:

Hypothesis 1: Small-to-medium-sized licensees tend to have had products in the declining stage of PLC.

Hypothesis 1 concerns small and medium-sized firms that are forced into bankruptcy because they do not have new and competitive technology, and their existing products(s) have reached the declining stage of the PLC. Acceptance of this hypothesis implies that these firms start their search for new technology once their existing technology reaches the declining stage of the PLC.

> *Hypothesis 2*: Small-to-medium-sized licensees are more likely to acquire a license to manufacture products whose manufacturing process (know-how) is related to that of their existing products (same product line, same process, or same standard industrial code [sic].

Hypothesis 2 says that small and medium-sized firms are more likely to purchase a technology directly related to their existing ones because they understand and absorb it better, faster, and at a lower cost. This might not be the case for large firms with different motives for taking a license (such as diversification).

> *Hypothesis 3*: Licensees with a high ration of scientists and engineers are more likely to acquire the license at an earlier stage in the IPLC than those with fewer scientists and engineers.

Naturally, when the licensee has technical competence, it will be in a position to acquire technology at an earlier stage of the PLC, where the risks are higher. Licensees without core skills have to acquire technology (product) at a later stage of the PLC, where technology has been commercially proven and the risks are lower. These licensees do not have the qualified personnel to understand, absorb, and adapt the technology at earlier stages.

> *Hypothesis 4*: Licensees with a high ratio of core skills (technically competent) tend to begin operations under license in environments of higher technical uncertainty than will those with a lower ratio or no such skills (technically noncompetent).

> *Hypothesis 5*: Technically competent licensees tend to take a license in environments of higher marketing uncertainty than will noncompetent licensees.

Hypotheses 4 and 5 stem directly from hypothesis 3, except that the focus of hypothesis 4 is on technical uncertainty and that of hypothesis 5 is on marketing uncertainty.

> *Hypothesis 6*: Dominant licensees are more likely to be able to negotiate a lower royalty rate and fewer

restrictions in the license agreement than are nondominant licensees.

Hypothesis 6 focuses on dominance characteristics of the licensee and the impact of such characteristics on the licensing compensation arrangements. It was stated earlier that when the licensee is the dominant party, the royalty fee paid to the licensor is lower or the restrictions imposed by the licensor are fewer. This is not the case for non-dominant licensees.

Hypothesis 7: Licensees with continuous license agreements are more likely to go through the licensing cycle than are those with one-time agreements, provided they gradually build their own in-house core skills.

When a licensee acquires technology on a continuous basis, the probability of dependence on the licensor exists, the probability of dependence on the licensor exists, although the likelihood is minimized if the licensee builds its own in-house competence (with the help of the licensor and the experience acquired while manufacturing under license). After the licensee has acquired the competence, the existing agreement with the licensor can be renegotiated and/or canceled. Such is not the case with one-time and "current technology" agreements. This hypothesis is a direct result of the LCM.

Hypothesis 8: License agreements on a continuous basis are more likely to have more restrictions, such as geographical and procurement, than are noncontinuous or one-time agreements.

Hypothesis 8 compares license agreement types. Obviously, when the agreement is on a continuous basis, the amount of information and assistance provided by the licensor to the licensee is much more greater than in one-time contracts. Consequently, the licensee has to compensate the licensor accordingly. The compensation may be in the form of higher licensing fees or the number of restrictions in the agreements.

Based on the research model and the hypotheses, the following tabulated distributions of licensees are expected. The expectations of the hypotheses are summarized in Tables 5.1 and 5.2. Note that L and M indicate the expected frequency of licensees in each cell.

TABLE 5.1 Summary of Research Hypotheses: Licensees' Characteristics

Licensees' Characteristics	Technology Life Cycle (Stage)		Type of Licensed Technology		Technical Uncertainty (degree)		Marketing Uncertainty (degree)		Royalty Rate (% of sales)		License Restrictions (number)	
	Earlier	Later	Related	Unrelated	Low	High	Low	High	Less Than 3%	More Than 3%	One or None	Two or More
Small	L (H1)	M	M	L	M	L	M	L	L	M	L	M
Large	M	L	L	M (H2)	L	M	L	M	M	L	M	L
With Core skills	M (H3)	L	L	M	L	M	L	M	M	L	M	L
Without core skills	L	M	M	L	M	L (H4)	M	L (H5)	L	M	L	M
Dominant	M	L	L	M	L	M	L	M	M (H6a)	L	M	L
Nondominant	L	M	M	L	M	L	M	L	L	M	L (H6b)	M

Note: L (less) or M (more) indicates number of firms in that cell.
Source: Based on original material compiled by the author.

TABLE 5.2 Summary of Hypotheses: Licensing Agreement Types

License Agreement Type	Cancellation of License by Licensee due to		Licensees' R&D Capabilities		Production Difficulty		Number of Restrictions	
	Patent Life/ Disagreement	Licensees' Competence	Decreased/ Unchanged	Increased	Decreased	Increased/ Unchanged	One or None	Two or More
Continuous	L	M	L	M	M	L	L	M
		H7a		H7b		H7c		H8
One-time	M	L	M	L	L	M	M	L

Notes: Less (L) and more (M) indicate number of firms in that cell.
Source: Based on original material compiled by the author.

6

The Research Methodology
and Design

THE RESEARCH METHODOLOGY

In order to carry out the research and empirically test the hypotheses (discussed in Chapter 5), there is a need to operationalize the hypotheses and put them in a statistically testable form. But before that, the sample, population, and research instrument are discussed.

Population and Sampling

The universe consists of all the licensees in the United States, and the sample consists of all the Ohio licensees. These Ohio licensees are some of the 4,038 Ohio manufacturing firms that participated in Prof. Lee C. Nehrt's survey of the *Ohio Exporter Directory*. One hundred forty-five of the participants had indicated that they were licensees to foreign licensors, but further investigation revealed that 27 were neither licensees nor manufacturers. The focus of this research is on manufacturing licensees.

Consequently, the sample consists of 118 Ohio manufacturing licensees. A complete list of these firms and their profiles are in the appendix.

Research Instrument

Since there is almost no literature on this special topic and there is no public information on international licensing of technology (for a good reason—trade secrets!), it was decided to use a questionnaire as the main research instrument. Interviews with ten licensees' executives were part of this process. After reviewing the literature (almost all of the literature on international licensing of technology has taken a licensor's standpoint—see Chapter 4), a comprehensive list of important issues in technology licensing (from the licensee's standpoint) was collected. Then consultation with various organizations (such as the Licensing Executive Society [L.E.S.]) and executives involved in international licensing of technology began; after six months a comprehensive questionnaire was designed. The goal was a questionnaire specific and operational enough to reveal answers to the research questions, yet general enough to entice the executives to answer the questions without revealing any privileged information or trade secrets. Overall, the process of selecting the appropriate questions and the questionnaire design were semi-delphi techniques, as discussed below.

Validity

Several measures were taken to ensure the validity of the instrument in terms of content and criterion-related material. First, a bank of about 100 items (issues) was gathered from the literature. Second, the bank was sorted out by a panel of eight judges who were professors or company executives involved in international technology licensing, to determine the appropriateness and length of the items in the questionnaire. Finally, the bank of items was sorted into categories of companies engaged in reverse licensing and factors that motivated such companies. A simple consensus determined which items were best representative of the identified subscales.

Reliability

The questionnaire was designed in a Likert scale form and was first sent to 50 randomly selected firms for a pilot study. The goal was to determine the reliability (replicability) of the questionnaire. The returned questionnaires were coded, tabulated, and examined for reliability and internal consistency of the survey instrument, using the split-half method in conjunction with the Spearman-Brown formula. The split-half method consisted of splitting the questionnaire items into 13 odd- and 13 even-numbered items. The halves were correlated, then the reliability of the whole instrument was determined by using the value of the correlation coefficient between the two halves (found with the Spearman-Brown formula). The value of the reliability coefficient was found to be 0.94, which indicates that the questionnaire was very reliable. (See Appendix 6.4 for calculations of reliability coefficient $[r^2]$).

THE STATISTICAL DESIGN AND DATA ANALYSIS

The Choice of Chi-Square as the Test Statistic

Because the data will be in the form of frequencies, and because the subsequent data analysis must involve the analysis of frequencies, the chi-square becomes the appropriate choice of test statistic. Chi-square is among the most popular statistical inference procedures today. It is typically easy to implement and can reveal a great many characteristics of a random variable or set of random variables. Chi-square is widely used for tests of independence and contingency tables, which are used to display the dependence of two or more variables. The hypotheses are tested for independence using their null form, which is basically the difference between the observed frequencies and the expected frequencies. With power of the chi-square test, one is able to discover the presence or absence of relationships among the research variables. Once a relationship is found, how can one determine the degree of intensity of that relationship or the strength of the association? In the next section, different measures of association will be introduced. The alpha level for statistical significance is 0.05.

The Choice of Gamma as
the Measure of Association

Among the commonly known measures of association, gamma has the advantage of being more sensitive to the differential distributions of the categories of independent variables. The contingency coefficient is not used because of two apparent weaknesses: (1) it has no sign, and (2) it never reaches 1 (one), and hence is not clearly interpretable (see Appendix 6.3 for more detailed analysis). Also, while lambda and tau both measure the relative reduction of errors in predicting the correct category of dependent variables, gamma measures the relative reduction of errors in predicting order on the dependent variable. The data in this study are ordinal data. Another advantage of gamma is that while its numerical value represents the strength of association, a positive sign indicates that the variables increase concomitantly, whereas a negative sign indicates that as one variable increases, the other decreases.

THE RELATIONSHIP BETWEEN THE RESEARCH HYPOTHESES AND THE RESEARCH INSTRUMENT

The first hypothesis deals with licensees' characteristics (size) and the characteristics of the licensed technology (PLC). This hypothesis is operationalized and translated into questions 3 (size) and 7 (PLC) of the questionnaire.

The second hypothesis translates into questions 3 (size) and 9 (type of licensed technology) of the questionnaire.

The third hypothesis focuses on licensees' characteristics (core skills) and the licensed technology characteristics (PLC). The related questions in the questionnaire 3c and 12(1) and 8.

The fourth and fifth hypotheses concern on licensees' characteristics (core skills) and the licensed technology characteristics (technical and marketing uncertainties). The related questions in the questionnaire are 3c and 12(1) and 12(2), respectively.

Hypothesis 6 focuses on licensees' characteristics (dominance) and the license agreement characteristics (royalty rate and restrictions). The related questions are 11, and 20 and 17, respectively.

Hypothesis 7 concerns the LCM and type of licensing agreement. The related questions in the questionnaire are 21, 23, and 16, respectively.

Finally, hypothesis 8 focuses on the type of licensing agreement (continuous or one-time, restrictions). The corresponding questions in the questionnaire are 16 and 17.

In Chapter 7, after checking the data gathered by the research instrument (questionnaire) with public and private sources (such as firms' reports) for accuracy, they will be tested by using test statistics introduced in this chapter. Also, the statistical results will be compared with the results from this researcher's interviews with Ohio licensees' executives. The objective is to compare the results for consistency between statistical findings and executives' perceptions, on the one hand, and to shed light on and to support the statistical analyses and interpretations, on the other.

APPENDIX 6.1   THE QUESTIONNAIRE

THE OHIO STATE UNIVERSITY

COLLEGE OF ADMINISTRATIVE SCIENCE

REVERSE LICENSING : The International Transfer of Technology in the U.S. (Ohio)

Company Name:

Product(s):

Ownership: Public [ ]
             Private [ ]

I.   GENERAL INFORMATION:

1.   Please indicate the phrase that best describes your INTERNATIONAL INTERESTS:

A company with:
[ ] Overseas manufacturing, sales and service facilities.
[ ] No overseas manufacturing BUT sales and service facilities.
[ ] Foreign agents or similar organizations.
[ ] Only domestic operations.

2.   Please indicate the EXTENT to which your company uses the following METHODS
     for finding opportunities for TRANSFER or ACQUISITION of technology.

	Very Great Ext.=5	Great Ext.=4	Some Ext.=3	Little Ext.=2	No Ext.=1
Personal contacts	[ ]	[ ]	[ ]	[ ]	[ ]
Trade & scientific publications, associations, and/or conventions	[ ]	[ ]	[ ]	[ ]	[ ]
U.S. (State) Government Assistance	[ ]	[ ]	[ ]	[ ]	[ ]
Foreign Government and/or International Institutions Assistance	[ ]	[ ]	[ ]	[ ]	[ ]
Licensing Brokers	[ ]	[ ]	[ ]	[ ]	[ ]
Direct market effort by your company	[ ]	[ ]	[ ]	[ ]	[ ]
Direct request from potential partner	[ ]	[ ]	[ ]	[ ]	[ ]
Other (please specify) _____	[ ]	[ ]	[ ]	[ ]	[ ]

3.   Please indicate the appropriate box(es) for your firm's SALES, EXPORTS, and
     NUMBER OF EMPLOYEES (1984 calendar year):

(a) Total Sales
     Under $5 million   [ ]
     Between $5-$25 million   [ ]
     Between $25-100 million   [ ]
     More than $100 million   [ ]

     Exports Sales
     Under $5 million   [ ]
     Between $5-$25 million   [ ]
     Between $25-100 million   [ ]
     More than $100 million   [ ]

(b) Number of employees
     Less than 100   [ ]
     Between 100-500   [ ]
     Between 500-1000   [ ]
     More than 1000   [ ]

(c) Number of scientists & engineers
     (core skills)

                                    Number
     At the time of licensing
     agreement (year: _____)   _____
     Now (1984)   _____

APPENDIX 6.1 Continued

II. LICENSING MOTIVATION(S):

4. Please rate the following in terms of their importance as <u>MOTIVE(S)</u> for
    international licensing of technology:

    (a) YOUR COMPANY'S MOTIVE(S):

	Most imp.	Very imp.	Some imp.	Little imp.	No imp.
1. To acquire the needed technology and/or to supplement your existing R & D	[ ]	[ ]	[ ]	[ ]	[ ]
2. To avoid the risk of R & D expenditures and/or acquire the technology not available in the United States	[ ]	[ ]	[ ]	[ ]	[ ]
3. To acquire the right to operate (patent) and/or to settle a patent dispute	[ ]	[ ]	[ ]	[ ]	[ ]
4. To diversify your operations (related and/or unrelated product lines)	[ ]	[ ]	[ ]	[ ]	[ ]
5. Other (please specify) _____	[ ]	[ ]	[ ]	[ ]	[ ]

    (b) YOUR LICENSOR'S MOTIVE(S): (in your opinion)

	Most imp.	Very imp.	Some imp.	Little imp.	No imp.
1. To extend the technology's life (declining in commerical uses and/or not used commercially in their home markets)	[ ]	[ ]	[ ]	[ ]	[ ]
2. To earn extra revenue not otherwise possible	[ ]	[ ]	[ ]	[ ]	[ ]
3. To enter the U.S. market but didn't have financial and/or marketing resources and expertise	[ ]	[ ]	[ ]	[ ]	[ ]
4. To establish and/or test the market for future investment	[ ]	[ ]	[ ]	[ ]	[ ]
5. Other (please specify) _____	[ ]	[ ]	[ ]	[ ]	[ ]

III. LICENSE AGREEMENT AND LICENSEE-LICENSOR RELATIONSHIP:

5. Please indicate HOME COUNTRY of licensor(s):

6. PRIOR to licensing agreement,

    [ ] You had no relationship with the licensor
    [ ] You were the licensor's distributor in the U.S.
    [ ] The licensor was your distributor (import agent)
    [ ] The licensor was a licensee to your other product (process)
    [ ] Other (Indicate) _____

7. Please indicate the phrase that describes your own other product(s) life
    cycle (not the licensed product) in the U.S. PRIOR to licensing agreement(s):

    [ ] R & D stage
    [ ] Early commercial stage (up to 5 years in the market)
    [ ] Mature stage (more than 5 years in commercial use)
    [ ] Declining in commercial use
    [ ] Other (Please specify) _____

APPENDIX 6.1   Continued

8. Please describe the phrase that best describes the <u>STAGE</u> that the licensed technology (product) had reached in the <u>LICENSOR'S</u> market, when you acquired the technology:

    [ ] R & D stage
    [ ] Early commercial stage (up to 5 years)
    [ ] Mature stage (in commerical use more than 5 years)
    [ ] Declining commercial use by the licensor
    [ ] No longer commercially used by licensor

9. Please COMPARE the licensed technology (product or process) with your firm's other products <u>PRIOR</u> to the licensing agreement and check the appropriate box(es):

    [ ] Similar to your other products (same line...same marketing channels)
    [ ] Uses same or similar manufacturing process as your other products
    [ ] Unrelated to your products or manufacturing processes
    [ ] Other (please specify) _____

10. Please indicate the phrase that best describes the <u>COMPETITIVE</u> nature of the <u>LICENSED TECHNOLOGY</u>: (in your opinion)

    (a) LICENSOR(S) MARKET
         [ ] The technology is (was) uniquely available from licensor.
         [ ] The technology is (was) available from FEW OTHERS.
         [ ] Similar technology is (was) available from SEVERAL OTHER SOURCES
              (technologically and economically competitive).
         [ ] Other technically or economically INFERIOR technology is (was)
              available from others.

    (b) LICENSEE(S) MARKET
         [ ] Your company was the ONLY applicant for the acquisition of licensed
              technology.
         [ ] There were FEW other applicants for the acquisition of licensed technology.
         [ ] There were SEVERAL applicants for the acquisition of licensed technology.

11. Please <u>COMPARE</u> your firm (as a licensee) with the licensor in terms of sales, number of employees, and R & D expenditures and check (x) the appropriate boxes:

	Sales	Employees	R & D Expenditure
Licensee is SMALLER than Licensor	[ ]	[ ]	[ ]
Licensee is EQUAL to Licensor	[ ]	[ ]	[ ]
Licensee is LARGER than Licensor	[ ]	[ ]	[ ]

12. Please indicate the technical and marketing <u>UNCERTAINTY</u> associated with the licensed technology when the license was executed (i.e. the uncertainties involved with a commercially-proven product are much LOWER than those of products which are not commercially-proven):

	Low	Medium	High
(1) Technical uncertainty was	[ ]	[ ]	[ ]
(2) Marketing uncertainty was	[ ]	[ ]	[ ]

13. Please indicate approximately how much initial capital investment was needed in order to begin the production under the license:

    Under $1 million   [ ]   Between $50-$100 million   [ ]
    Between $1-$10 million   [ ]   More than $100 million   [ ]
    Between $10-$50 million   [ ]

APPENDIX 6.1   Continued

14. Please indicate <u>WHAT</u> was (were) acquired by the licensing agreement(s):

[ ] Patent rights (manufacturing rights)
[ ] Patent rights plus know-how (technical assistance)
[ ] Other (Please specify) _____

15. Please indicate your products <u>PRIOR</u> to licensing as well as your licensed-product(s) or process(es):

Prior Product(s): _____
.
Licensed Product(s): _____

16. Please indicate the <u>TYPE</u> of licensing agreement(s):

[ ] One-time transfer of technology
[ ] Continuous transfer of technology
[ ] Other (indicate) _____

17. Please indicate the <u>RESTRICTION(S)</u> contained in the agreement(s). (Check all applicable.)

[ ] Geographical restrictions
[ ] Procurement restriction
[ ] Cross licensing (Grant back)
[ ] Other (indicate) _____

IV. COMPENSATION & LICENSING IMPACTS

18. Please check the phrase(s) that describe the <u>COMPENSATION</u> arrangements associated with the license. (Check all applicable.)

[ ] **Percent of sales or volume**   [ ] Maximum payment
[ ] **Minimum Annual payments**   [ ] Raw materials
[ ] **Lump sum payment**   [ ] Licensed product(s)
[ ] **Graduated decreasing royalty**   [ ] Other product(s)
[ ] **Graduated increasing royalty**   [ ] Other (specify) _____

19. **Please indicate the percentage of your firm's sales revenue generated by the licensed product, percentage of your net sales spent on R & D, and the number of licensing agreements:**

	Licensing Agreement Year: _____	1984
% of sales from licensed product	[ ]	[ ]
% of net sales spent on R & D	[ ]	[ ]
Number of licensing agreements	[ ]	[ ]

20. **Please indicate the <u>approximate cost</u> of acquiring technology (licensed product or process), as a percentage of your sales revenue from the licensed product (process):**

[ ] **Under 3%**   [ ] Between 8% – 10%
[ ] **Between 3% – 5%**   [ ] Between 10% – 15%
[ ] **Between 5% – 8%**   [ ] More than 15%

APPENDIX 6.1 Continued

21. Please check the appropriate box(es) for the following:

During the time your firm has been producing under license,

	Decreased	Unchanged	Increased
Production difficulties associated with it	[ ]	[ ]	[ ]
Profit margin associated with it	[ ]	[ ]	[ ]
Your R & D capabilities	[ ]	[ ]	[ ]
Your dependence on the licensor (for current & future technology)	[ ]	[ ]	[ ]

22. Please check the degree to which the technology transfer (license) IMPACTED on the following factors in the United States (Ohio):

	Greatly Increased	Increased	Neutral	Decreased	Greatly Decreased
(1) Number of low skill jobs	[ ]	[ ]	[ ]	[ ]	[ ]
(2) Number of high skill jobs	[ ]	[ ]	[ ]	[ ]	[ ]
(3) Number of managerial jobs	[ ]	[ ]	[ ]	[ ]	[ ]
(4) Export potentials	[ ]	[ ]	[ ]	[ ]	[ ]
(5) Use of domestic raw materials & products	[ ]	[ ]	[ ]	[ ]	[ ]
(6) Substitution for imported goods & products	[ ]	[ ]	[ ]	[ ]	[ ]
(7) Quality of environment, etc.	[ ]	[ ]	[ ]	[ ]	[ ]
(8) Other (specify) _____	[ ]	[ ]	[ ]	[ ]	[ ]

23. Please indicate whether you are producing any product(s) or utilizing any process(es) NOW that was (were) under license previously, but the license has expired or has been cancelled.   [ ] Yes   [ ] No

If yes, please choose the phrase that best describes WHY the license was cancelled (not renewed):

[ ] The patent legal protection (life) had expired.

[ ] A disagreement with licensor with regard to marketing and compensations.

[ ] The licensed technology was becoming obsolete and/or non-competitive and we had acquired competence to develop our own technology.

[ ] The cancellation of the licensing agreement was part of our STRATEGIC PLANNING and as soon as we had achieved the technical capabilities, we did not need any foreign assistance.

[ ] Other (please specify) _____

24. Do you desire to receive a copy of the research results? [ ] Yes   [ ] No

THANK YOU FOR YOUR CONSIDERATION.

APPENDIX 6.2 Profile of Ohio Licensees Surveyed

COMPANY NAME & ADDRESS	PRODUCTS	SIC#	EMPL.	ANNUAL SALES	CHIEF EXECUTIVES
* 1. A & F Machine Prdts. Co. 454 Geiger St. Berea, OH 44017	Chemical Treatment pumps	3561	20	1.1-5mm Export	Fred J. Helwig/Pres. Fred Helwig Jr./V.P.
* 2. ADB Almaco Inc. 977 Gahanna Pkwy. P.O. Box 30829 Columbus, OH 43230	Airport Lighting & Navigation Equipment	3648	80	5.1-10mm Rsch.	Gary P. Weltlich/Pres.
* 3. Ardell, Inc. 30601 Carter Road Solon, OH 44139	Hair care products	2844	150	10.1-25mm Rsch. facilities Import Export	Arnold M. Miller/Pres. Lydell Miller/V.P.
4. Atlas Copco Jarva Inc. 29125 Hall St. Solon, OH 44139	Tunnel boring machines,	3531	80	10.1-25mm Rsch. facilities Import	Luke Home/Pres. Michael Antochow/Sales
* 5. Avco New Idea Farm Eqpt. 420 S. 1st St. Coldwater, OH 45828	Farm Implements	3523	1200	Over 25mm Import Export	C. J. Stralow/G/Mgr. R. W. McCormic/Sales
* 6. BTL of Ohio 2112 Sylvan Ave. P.O. Box 2570 Toledo, OH 43606	Formaldehyde & Melamine Formaldehyde Adhesives	2891	33	1.1-5mm Rsch facilities Export	
7. Hurres FECO Division of Bangor Punta Operations 5855 Grant Ave.	Industrial heating Eqpt. ovens, conveyors, sheet metal brakes & dryers	3567	100	5.1-10mm Export	Helmut Deichmann/Pres. James D. Anderson/V.P.

APPENDIX 6.2 Continued

COMPANY NAME & ADDRESS	PRODUCTS	SIC#	EMPL.	ANNUAL SALES	CHIEF EXECUTIVES
Cleveland, OH 44105					
* 8. Barneby-Cheney Co. 835 N. Cassaday Ave. P.O. Box 2526 Columbus, OH 43216	Activated carbon purification & recovery equipment	3569	70	1.1-5mm Rsch. facilities Imports Exports	William Clark/Pres. William Vogel/V.P.
9. Bendix Automation & Measurement Division 721 Springfield P.O. Box 1127 Dayton, OH 45401	Dimensional measuring gages, form grinders	3345	400	Over 25mm Rsch. facilities Export	Kevin Carey/Mkt. Mgr. B. Skeleton/Pl. Mgr.
10. Bisphoric Products Co. 4413 Kings Run Rd. Cincinnati, OH 45232	Steel lined & stainless steel tanks, applicators	3551	250	Over 25mm Exports	A. E. Hucke/Pres. A. Roehr/V.P.
11. Blaney Lumber Union St. P.O. Box 8 Bethesda, OH 43719	Treated lumber, machinery mats, blocking	2421	63	1.1-5mm Exports	D. Blaney/ R. Blaney/Owners
* 12. Bry-Air, Inc. Rte. 37W, P.O. Box 269 Sunbury, OH 43074	Dehumidifiers, Industrial Environmental control systems, plastic drying & conveying equipment	3443	60	5.1-10mm Rsch. facilities Export	P. D. Griesse/Pres. S. D. Fitch/V.P.
13. Bryan Metals Inc. 1103 S. Main St. P.O. Box 487	Copper & Copper alloy strip	3351	60	Export	R. W. Polland/Pres. Rex R. Dale/V.P.

Bryan, OH 43506

#	Company	Products	Code	Empl.	Facilities/Sales	Officers
14.	Buckhorn Material Handling Group 10605 Chester Road Cincinnati, OH 45215	Materials handling, containers & allied equipment for industrial commercial food & institutional applications	3076	100	N.A.	Richard Johnston/Pres. Robert J. Goosman/V.P.
15.	Buckhorn 3592 Corporate Dr. Columbus, OH 43216	Materials handling, containers & allied equipment for industrial commercial food & institutional applications.	3079	1000	over $25 mill.	
16.	Campbell Hausfeld Co. Melbev Energy Systems Div. 100 Production Frive Harrison, OH 45030	Tanks, ASME Code-non code & propane	3443	350	10.1mm-25mm	Robert L. Hergert/GMgr. Joe MacFarland/Sales
17.	Canfield Industry, Inc. 3632 Western Reserve Canfield, OH 44406	Solenoid valve pilots, pneumatic control valves & electronics	3494	10	501m-1mm Rsch. facilities Export Import	John Rasmussen/Pres.
* 18.	Chardon Rubber Co. 373 Washington St. Chardon, OH 44024	Molded & extruded rubber & plastic products	3069	600	10.1-25mm Rsch. facilities Export	J. W. Keener/JR. Pres. Don W. Sullivan/V.P.
* 19.	Cincinnati Gear Co. 5657 Wooster Pike Cincinnati, OH 45227	Gears & gear assemblies	3566	300	10.1-25mm Import Export	Walter L. Rye/Pres. W. Gay/V.P.
20.	Cleveland Twist Drill Co. Sub. Acme Cleveland Corp.	Drills, reamers, end mills, carbide	3545	2100	Rsch. facilities Export	James T. Bartlett/Pres. R. Russell/V.P.

APPENDIX 6.2 Continued

COMPANY NAME & ADDRESS	PRODUCTS	SIC#	EMPL.	ANNUAL SALES	CHIEF EXECUTIVES
1242 E. 49 St. P.O. Box 6656 Cleveland, OH 44101	cutting tools				
* 21. Cleveland Vibrator Co. 2828 Clinton Ave. Cleveland, OH 44113	Air & electric vibrators & vibrating	3532	55	5.1mm-10mm Rsch. facilities Export	D. Robichard/Pres. J. Tesar/V.P.
* 22. Coe Manufacturing Co. 609 Bank St., P.O. Box 520 Painesville, OH 44077	Vaneer lathes & dryers, fiber & plasterboard equipment	3541	350	10.1mm-25mm Rsch. facilities	Fred W. Fields/Pres. George B. Milbourne/ Sales Mgr.
* 23. Consolidated Cermaic Prdts. 838 Cherry St. Blanchester, OH 45107	Ceramic coated fluxing pipe, protection tubes & thermocouples for alum. ind. & hot top boards & tundish lines for steel industry	3479	200	5.1mm-10mm Export	R. Bruce Mickey/Pres. Gary F. Meyer/V.P.
24. Cor Tec Inc. Sub. UMC Ind. 2351 Kenskill Ave. Washington Court House, OH 43160	Fiberglass reinforced plywood panels	3292	180	Over 25mm Export	N.A.
* 25. Cosmicoat, Inc. 3400 Cleveland Rd. P.O. Box 73 Wooster, OH 44691	Pavement maintenance & tennis court coatings	2891	33	5.1mm-10mm Export Import	Donald J. Harris/Pres. Richard R. Benson/V.P.

#	Company	Product	Code	Emp.	Trade	Officers
26.	Crowley Co. 14623 Forest Ridge P.O. Box 281 Newbury, OH 44065	Air moving equipment	3564	10	501mm-25mm Import Export	James J. Crowley/Pres. T. W. Crowley/V.P.
27.	Day Mixing Taylor Stiles 4932 Beech St. Cincinnati, OH 45212	Industrial mixers, size reduction equipment engineered systems, waste reclamation systems	3559	120	10.1mm-25mm Rsch. facilities Export	Joseph G. Weger/Pres. Robert Miller/V.P.
*28.	Dayton Barsplitch Inc. 1875 Radio Rd. P.O. Box 31308 Dayton, OH 45431	Miscellaneous metal work	3449	80	N.G.	N.A.
29.	Dayton Superior Corp. 721 Richard St. Miamisburg, OH 45342	Accessories & hardware for the forming of concrete & concrete chemicals, contract manu.	3429	550	Over 25mm Import Export	Glen P. Schimpf/Pres. Thomas M. Carroll/Sales
*30.	Dupps Co. 548 N. Cherry P.O. Box 95 Germantown, OH 45327	Process machinery	3551	185	10.1mm-25mm Export	John A. Dupps/Pres. John A. Dupps Jr./V.P.
31.	Dyson, Joseph & Sons Inc. 53 Freedom Road P.O. Box 228 Painesville, OH 44077	Lift truck forks, large threaded	3462	250	Rsch. facilities Export	Rochard Crosby/Pres. Richard W. Foss/V.P.
32.	Eagle-Pitcher Ind. Akron Standard Div. 1624 Englewood	Machinery molds for rubber & plastic industries	3559	240	Over 25mm Rsch. Import Export	L. Mulhollen/Pres. J. Segatta/V.P.

APPENDIX 6.2 Continued

COMPANY NAME & ADDRESS	PRODUCTS	SIC#	EMPL.	ANNUAL SALES	CHIEF EXECUTIVES
P.O. Box 1869 Akron, OH 44309					
* 33. Eaton Corp. Airflex Div. 9919 Clinton Road Cleveland, OH 44144	Air activated magnetic, hydraulic clutches & brakes	3568	400	Rsch. facilities Export	Ray Mack/Gen. Mgr. Robert L. Burks/Sales
34. Elu Machinery Co. 9040 Dutton Dr. Twinsburg, OH 44087	Metalworking machinery	3451	20	1.1mm-5mm Export	Eugen Lutz/Pres. Joachim Scholt/Pl. Mgr.
35. Erickson Tool Co. Div. Kennametal Inc. 34300 Solon Road Solon, OH 44139	Machine tool accessories & carbide cutting tools	3545	350	Rsch. facilities Import Export	Quentin McKenna/Pres. Bill Eversole/V.P.
* 36. Etna Products, Inc. 16824 Park Circle Dr. POB 286 Chagrin Falls, OH 44022	Indl. extreme pressure lubricants & systems dispensing lubricants reclamation of drawing oils, hydraulic oils, rolling oils	2992	20	1.1-5mm Rsch. facilities Import Export	Ike Tripp, Sr./Pr. Ike Tripp, Jr./V.P.
37. Euclid Inc. Daimler-Benz AG. 22221 St. Clair Ave. Euclid, OH 44117	Earth moving trucks	3531	800	Over 25mm. Rsch. Export	Juergen Schrempp/Pres. Harvey Lebarron/V.P.

#	Company / Address	Products	Code	Empl.	Size / Facilities	Officers
38.	Exomet Inc. Maple Ave. POB 647 Conneaut, OH 44030	Exothermic insulating products, heat treating eqpt. & supplies	2899	50	5.1mm-10mm Rsch. facilities Import Export	D. Wearn/Pres. M. McFann/V.P.
* 39.	Fairfield Engineering 324 Barnhart St. POB 526 Marion, OH 43302	Conveying & handling eqpt. for steel industry, for rubber coal, glass, foundry	3535	450	Over 25mm Export	
* 40.	Ferry Inds. Inc. 1050 W. Main St. POB 299 Kent, OH 44240	Die cutters, foam fbrcg. Special machinery builders, automation, rubber test eqpt.	3559	65	1.1-5mm Export Import	W. Harry Covington/Pres.
* 41.	Flexiblast Co. 985 W. Locust St. Wilmington, OH 45177	Mechanical wire descaler, custom built machinery	3549	8	501m-1mm Export	H. Steel Price, III/Pr.
* 42.	Forma Scientific Inc. Mill Creek Road POB 649 Marietta, OH 45750	Environmental cabinets, lab eqpt. furniture, incubators baths, freezers, ovens	3811	312	10.1mm-25mm Rsch. facilities Import Export	Byron Westerman/V.P.
* 43.	Fostoria Inds., Inc. General Prdts. Div. 1200 N. Main POB E Fostoria, OH 44830	Gas & electric infrared eqpt., indl. & commercial lighting elec. infrared	3567	175	5.1mm-10mm Rsch. facilities Export	E. N. Schalk/Pr. R. E. Justice/V.P.
44.	General Motors Corp. Inland Div. 2701 Home Ave. POB 1224 Dayton, OH 45401	Strg. wheels, brakehose lining, ball joints, weather-strips, E. P. pads engine & trans. mounts, foam seat pads	3714	4964	Over 25mm Rsch. facilities Export	L. P. Roberts/Gen. Mgr. G. F. Richards/Sls. Mgr.

APPENDIX 6.2 Continued

COMPANY NAME & ADDRESS	PRODUCTS	SIC#	EMPL.	ANNUAL SALES	CHIEF EXECUTIVES
45. G. F. Business Eqpt. 229 E. Dennick Ave. Youngstown, OH 44501	Desk files, shelving, contract metalwork, seating, open plan system	2522	1200	Over 25mm Rsch. facilities Import Export	Ronald R. Anderson/Pr. Ronald G. Statz/V.P.
46. Gilford Instrument Labs.,Inc. 132 Artino St. Oberlin, OH 44074	Spectro-phono-meters, chemistry analyzers	3841	750	Over 25mm Rsch. facilities Export	Richard Dunn/Pr. A. A. Caprio/Sls. Mgr.
47. Global Drilling Suppliers, Inc. POB 67 Harrison, OH 45030	Water well drilling eqpt.	3440	5	0-1m	Ted W. Walker
48. Gugan Machine Corp. 1440 E. 55th St. Cleveland, OH 44103	Hardness testing machinery, spring forming machinery	3559	60	1-1.5mm Export	
49. Hobart Bros. Co. 600 W. Main St. Troy, OH 45373	Air welding systs., industrial battery chargers, aircraft ground power units	3623	1500	Over 25mm Rsch. facilities Import Export	William H. Hobart/Pr. R. B. Bravo/V.P.
50. Hollander Industries 219 Kelley Ave. Dayton, OH 45404	Aluminum die casting	3362	150	10.1mm-25mm Rsch. facilities Import Export	Irvin Hollander/Pr. Larry Hollander/V.P.
51. Huffy Corp. Ohio Bicycle Div. 410 Grand Lake Rd.	Bicycles	3751	393	Import Export	J. Mariotti/Pr. W. Rapp/V.P.

Celina, OH 45822

#	Company	Products			Contact
52.	Inryco Inc. Spec. Prdts., Gp-Milco 1101 E. Kibby St. Lima, OH 45804	Door hatches, tele-scoping doors, acess doors	3447	137	Thomas Konopasek/ Gen. Mgr.
53.	Intercole Bolling Corp. 5500 Walworth Ave. Cleveland, OH 44102	Machinery for rubber plastics & metal forming industries	3559	100 10.1mm-25mm Export	James T. Matsuoka/ Gen. Mgr.
* 54.	John Zubal Inc. 2969 W. 25th St. Cleveland, OH 44113	Bookstores	5942	10 125,000 est. financial strength	John T. Zubal Owner/Mgr.
* 55.	Kaiser Aluminum & Chemicals Corp./Refractories Div. 41738 Easterly Dr. POB 47 Columbiana, OH 44408	Basic refractory brick (cement, mortars & mixers)	3297	1700 10.1mm-25mm Export	J. Allen Plant Mgr.
* 56.	Kern-Liebers USA Inc. Spring Div. 1510 Albon Rd. POB 396 Holland, OH 43528	Mainsprings, constant force springs, spiral torsion springs & fine blankings	3495	90 1.1-5mm Export	Lethan A. Bayrle/Pr. Hans Stein/V.P.
57.	Kernells Automatic Machining 8 W. Main St., POB 41 Berlin Hgts., OH 44814	Machine Products	3451	30 501m-1mm Export	Claude Kernell/Pr.
* 58	Koehring Morgan/Unit AMCA Int'l 947 E. Broadway Alliance, OH 44601	Cranes, heavy weld-ments, auxiliary mill equipment & presses	3536	750 Over 25mm. Export	J. R. Stadelman/Pr. G. L. Everhand/V.P.

APPENDIX 6.2 Continued

COMPANY NAME & ADDRESS	PRODUCTS	SIC#	EMPL.	ANNUAL SALES	CHIEF EXECUTIVES
59. Koppers Co., Inc. Bldg. Materials Div. 30060 Lakeland Blvd. Wickliffe, OH 44092	Tar coated glass, tar saturated cotton & jute glass mats, cold pro-cessed roofing materials, single piled roof systs.	2952	50	5.1-10mm Export	Merrilin McCarty/ Pur. Ag. R. E. Palent/Plt. Mgr.
* 60. Liason Int'l Inc. 1440 Fountains Springfield, OH 45504	Paper machinery & Office equipment	5051	50	300,000-499,000 est. financial strength	N.A.
* 61. LeBlond Machine Tool Madison & Edward Rd. Cincinnati, OH 45208	Lathes, standard & numerical control, machine tools	3541	1000	Over $25 mm Rsch. facilities Import Export	D. W. LeBlond/Pr. John Schultel/V.P.
62. Ledex, Inc. 801 Scholz Dr. POB 427 Vandalia, OH 45377	Positioning & switching prdts. manual & PB switches	3679	500	10.1-25mm Rsch. facilities Import Export	Gerald Leland/Pr. Charles Berthy/V.P.
* 63. Libbey-Owens Ford Co. Glass Div.	Float Glass: automotive and architectural	3231	5000	Over 25mm Export	R. W. Skeddle/Pr. B. R. Bush/V.P.
* 64. Liquid Control Corp. 7576 Freedom Ave., NW North Canton, OH 44720	Precision liquid dis-pensing eqpt., two components meter-mix-dispense machines	3559	22	1.1-5mm Rsch. facilities Import Export	William C. Schiltz/Pr. William A. Deneen/V.P.
* 65. Lodge & Shipley Co. 3055 Colerain Ave. Cincinnati, OH 45225	Lathes, CNC turning systems	3541	465	Over 25mm Import Export	W. L. Dolle, Jr./Pr. Roy M. Nelson/V.P.

Company	Products			Size/Facilities	Contact
* 66. Loopco Industries, Inc. 1981 E. Aurora Rd. Twinsburg, OH 44087	Slitting lines; coil handling, strip, processing eqpt; tube pipe mill auxiliary eqpt. end finishes	3559	70	10.1mm-25mm Export	Ken Smith/V.P.
67. Lordstown Rubber Co. 5232 Tod Ave., SW Warren, OH 44481	Rubber covered rollers & rubber linings, applicator rubber, pipe, tanks, tank cars	3069	33	1.1-5mm Rsch. facilities	Richard DeCamp/Gen. Mgr.
* 68. Lorenz Industries Lorenz Publishing	Printing of sacred and secular music	2751	68	1.1-5mm Export	S. Lorenz/Owners G. Lorenz/Owners
69. Mantaline Corp. 4754 E. High St. Mantua, OH 44255	Precision extruded rubber products	3069	170	Rsch. facilities Import Export	R. L. Merian/Pr. J. L. Klawitter/V.P.
70. MCB Reagants/ Aff. E. Mereck 2909 Highland Ave. Cincinnati, OH 45212	Laboratory chemicals, indicators, solvents & mineral acids	2899	120	10.1mm-25mm Rsch. facilities Import Export	Art Summerville/Pr. Michael M. Mulligan/V.P.
71. McPherson & Co. 227 Depot St. POB 92 Berea, OH 44017	Industrial glass	3211	13	Export	K. E. MacPherson/Pr.
72. Mannesmann Demay Corp. Mtrl. Handling Div. 29201 Aurora Rd. Solon, OH 44139	Hoists, cranes stacker systems motors	3536	275	Over 25mm Import Export	Wilbert J. Perch/V.P.
73. Manurhin Machine Tool Inc.	CNC screw machines	3441	20	5.1mm-10mm	William Ackerman/

APPENDIX 6.2 Continued

COMPANY NAME & ADDRESS	SIC#	EMPL.	ANNUAL SALES	PRODUCTS	CHIEF EXECUTIVES
(DST) Div. Mitac Corp. 11270 Grooms Rd. Cincinnati, OH 45242			Import		Gen. Mgr.
* 74. Masstron Scale Inc. 550 Shrock Rd. Columbus, OH 43229	3576	75	$1-5m	Scales & balances, except laboratory	Ben Dillon/Pres.
75. Mayfran Intl. Div. Fischer Inds. 6650 Beta Dr. POB 43038 Cleveland, OH 44143	3535	350	10.1mm-25mm Export	Conveyors, conveyor- belting, chip handling & processing systs. & paper & refuse handling eqpt.	Lawrence R. Fischer/Pr. Bruce Terry/V.P.
* 76. McGean-Rohco, Inc. 3203 W. 71st St. Cleveland, OH 44113	2819	200	5-10mm Rsch. facilities Export	Electroplating processes, inorganic, surface preparation, metalworking & trans. cleaning chemicals	D. L. Whitney/Pres. J. E. Vamos/V.P.
77. McNeil Akron Inc. Sub. EMS 96 E. Crosier St. Akron, OH 44311	3559	100	Over 25mm Rsch. facilities Import Export	Rotocast, vulcanizing, presses for tire industry rubber curing machinery	J. L. Gibney/Pres. W. Harry Covington, Jr./ V.P.
78. Midland-Ross Corp. Surface Division 2375 Dorr St., P.O. Box 907 Toledo, OH 43691	3567	330	Over 25mm Rsch. facilities	Industrial furnances & waste disposal systems	J. B. Andrews/V.P.

	Product				Officers
79. Monarch Sidney 615 N. Oak Sidney, OH 45365	Precision metal turning lathes, machining centers	3541	400	Over 25mm Rsch. facilities Export	Tony Niemeyer/Pres.
80. Namco Controls Division 7567 Tyler Blvd. Mentor, OH 44060	Industrial switches & solenoids, electrical controls	3699	195	10.1mm-25mm Rsch. facilities Export	Norman Swanson/Pres. Larry Ward/V.P.
* 81. North American Refractories E. 14th & Euclid Hanna Building Cleveland, OH 44115	Refractories	3255	1400	Over $25 mm Rsch. facilities Import Export	Edmond Wright/Pres. H. P. Berry/V.P.
82. Nutro Machinery Co. 3764 Ridge Road Cleveland, OH 44144	Automatic spray machines for painting & glazing	3559	20	1.1-5mm Export	R. M. Tomosko/V.P. Jochen Grocke/Gen. Mgr.
* 83. Ohio Art Co./Emenee 720 E. High P. O. Box 111 Bryan, OH 43506	File boxes, metal lithographed, toys trays	3944	600	Over 25mm Rsch. facilities Import Export	W. H. Martens/V.P. Wm. C. Killgallon/Pres.
84. Overhead Door Corp. Todco Division 1332 Fairground Rd. E. Marion, OH 43302	Upward acting doors for trucks & trailers, hydraulic tailgates, towing units	3536	150	5.1mm-10mm Export	R. C. Haugh/Pres. John Dahl/V.P.
85. Owens-Illinois Inc. Trading Co. 1 Sea Gate Toledo, OH 43666	Closures for plastic & glass containers prescription plastic vials, metal container lids	3466	3000	Over 25mm Rsch. facilities Import Export	W. F. Spengler/Pres. W. T. Hardy/V.P.
* 86. Owens-Illinois Inc. 1 Sea Gate	Glass tumblers, stemware, blown glass	3229	2200	Over 25mm Export Import	Robert J. Lanigan/Pres.

APPENDIX 6.2 Continued

COMPANY NAME & ADDRESS	PRODUCTS	SIC#	EMPL.	ANNUAL SALES	CHIEF EXECUTIVES
Toledo, OH 43666					
87. Pennwalt Corp. 421 London Rd., P.O. Box 363 Delaware, OH 43015	Cleaners, sanitizers, metal treating materials	2899	40	1.1-5mm Export Import	R. Riley/Oper. Mgr.
88. Pollock Co. Sub. Gatx Co. 101 Andrews Ave. P.O. Box 58 Youngstown, OH 44501	Blast furnace steel work, hot metal & slag handling equipment & heavy plate fabrication	3443	300	10.1-25mm Export	B. L. Shultz/V.P. Tom Butryn/Sales Mgr.
89. Polymer Raymond Inds. Inc. 15730 S. Madison P.O. Box 767 Middlefield, OH 44062	Molded & extruded rubber parts	3069	150	10.1-25mm Export	Ronald Raymond/Pres. Bing Medina/V.P.
90. Popped-Right Inc. 135 Wyandot Ave. P.O. Box 687 Marion, OH 43302	Snack foods	2099	125	10.1-25mm Export	D. Warren Brown/Pres. Ray Maloney/V.P.
91. Presision Metal Products Inc. 15411 Chatfield Cleveland, OH 44111	Metal stamping & assemblies	3469	20	501m-1mm Export	Thomas Jacin/Pres.
* 92. Pressure Systems Inc. 340 Enon Rd. Enon, OH 44111	General industrial machinery equipment Hydrolic Valve	3443	15	Below $1mm	Douglas E. Arnon/Pres.
* 93. Protective Treatments Inc.	Adhesives, sealants	2821	350	Over 25mm	C. W. Mercurio/Pres.

Company	Products			Officers
Helene Curtis Inds. Inc. 3345 Stop 8 Rd. P.O. Box 14116 Dayton, OH 45414	(liquids & extruded tape) plastisols, custom extrusions		Rsch. facilities Export	D. P. Riggle/V.P.
* 94. Questor Juvenile Furn. Co. 1801 Commerce Dr. Piqua, OH 45356	Crib mattresses, nursery pads, jubenile car seats & travel beds, tables framed high-chairs & play yards, strollers	2512	1412	Over 25mm Rsch. facilities Export	D. F. Mitchell/Pres. Allen Seymor/Sales
* 95. Race Chemical Equip. Corp. 6883 S. Ridge Rd. P.O. Box 115 Unionville, OH 44088	Industrial dialyzers, dialyzer membranes	3559	4	Under 100m Rsch. facilities Imports Exports	Richard Oldani/Pres. Peter M. Oldani/V.P.
96. Ral-Partha Enterprises 5938 Carthage Ct. Cincinnati, OH 45212	Metal figurines	3369	48	1.1-5mm Export	Jack Hesselbeck/Pres.
* 97. Sandusky Foundry & Mch. Co. 615 W. Market St. P.O. Box 1281 Sandusky, OH 44870	Job shop tools, job NC lathes, NC mill	3325	350	10.1mm-25mm Export	Charles Raiger/Pres. E. McPhillamy/V.P.
98. Schindler Haughton Elevator Co. P.O. Box 780 Toledo, OH 43695	Elevators	3534	570	Rsch. facilities Export	M. T. Wennerbom/JR.P.
* 99. SCM-Glidden Int'l Co. 925 Euclid Ave. Cleveland, OH 44115	Paints, typewriters, food chemical, emulsifiers	3389	3000	20-50mm	G. K. Brewin/V.P.

APPENDIX 6.2 Continued

COMPANY NAME & ADDRESS	PRODUCTS	SIC#	EMPL.	ANNUAL SALES	CHIEF EXECUTIVES
100. Seaforth Mineral & Ore Co., Inc. 29525 Chagrin Blvd. Pepper Pike, OH 44122	Coal & other minerals ores	5052	150	Over $25 m	N.A.
*101. Shreiner Sole Co. Taylor Dr. P.O. Box 347 Killbuck, OH 44637	Crepe rubber soles & plastic heels	3069	110	501m-1mm Rsch. facilities Export	V. E. Shreiner/Pres. Patrick W. Roche/V.P.
102. A. Schulman, Inc. 3550 W. Market St. Akron, OH 44313	Proprietary, custom plastic compounds, thermo-plastic resins, high & low polyethelene, polypropylene, monomer, PVC nylon	2821	50	Over 25mm Rsch. facilities Import Export	
*103. Spartan Chemical Co. 110 N. Westwood Ave. Toledo, OH 43607	Polishes & sanitation goods	2842	380	5.1-25mm Export	Eugene T. Swigart/Pres. T. J. Swigart/V.P.
104. Square & Co./Middletown Plant 1500 S. University Blvd. Middletown, OH 45042	Electrical equipment	3699	467	10.1-25mm Rsch. facilities Import Export	Bob Mattingly/Sales
*105. Steward-Glapat Corp. 1637 Moxahala P.O. Box 2486 Zanesville, OH 43701	Material handling equipment units	3535	40	1.1-5mm Exports	C. T. Stewart, Jr./Pres.
*106. Stroktol Co. of America 201 E. Steels Corner Rd.	Chemicals for rubber industry	2891	28	1.1-5mm Import Export	H. J. Bennett/Gen. Mgr.

Stow, OH 44224

No.	Company / Address	Products	SIC	Empl.	Notes	Officers
*107.	Sunstone Corp. 1500 Marguard Ave. P.O. Box 763 Cambridge, OH 43725	Ceramic products	3251	280	1.1-5mm Rsch. facilities	Spiro W. Bass/Pres. Philip J. Rich/Ch. Brd.
108.	Service Recorder Co. Sycon Corp. 959 Cheney Marion, OH 43302	Time & speed recorders, paper charts for recorders, fuel meters	3823	175	1.1-5mm Rsch. facilities Import Export	A. B. Siemer/Pres. Brendon Rocks/V.P.
109.	TLT-Babcock Inc. 411 Independence Dr. Medina, OH 44256	Axle & radial fans, large ventilating systems, silencing equipment & wind tunnels	3999	20	1.1-5mm Rsch. facilities	Michael J. Hug/Pl. Mgr.
110.	TPF Inc. 313 S. Wayne Ave. Cincinnati, OH 45215	Instrumentation, industrial dial	3823	6	Rsch. facilities Export	Robert Stiens/Pres. Chuch Stiens/Sales
*111.	Tecmar Inc. 23600 Mercantile Rd. Cleveland, OH 44122	Microprocessors & systems	3573	50	Rsch. facilities Export	Martin Alpert/Pres. Dave Wertman/V.P.
112.	Tremco Inc. 10701 Shaker Blvd. Cleveland, OH 44104	Protective coating & sealants for building maintenance & construction plus sealant for industry	2952	1250	Over 25mm Rsch. facilities Export	Leigh Carter/Pres.
113.	Trupar Inc. 2901 W. 3rd St. Dayton, OH 45417	Pumps & water systems, softeners	3561	16	101-250m Export	J. A. Sedlock/Pres.

APPENDIX 6.2 Continued

COMPANY NAME & ADDRESS	PRODUCTS	SIC#	EMPL.	ANNUAL SALES	CHIEF EXECUTIVES
114. United Technologies Wlliot Div. Carrier Corp. 1760 Tuttle Ave. P.O. Box 1165 Dayton, OH 45401	Rolelr burnishing tools, tube expanders & cutters machine systems	3542	75	5.1mm-10mm Import Export	Roy B. Pleiman/V.P.
*115. United Technologies Elliot Co. 1809 Sheridan Ave. Springfield, OH 45501	Tube maintenance tubes	3599	105	5.1mm-10mm Rsch. facilities Import Export	Wm. C. Sears/V.P.
116. Universal Metal Prdts. Inc. 29980 Lakeland Blvd. Wickliffe, OH 44092	Heat treating & finishing, small stamping	3398	125	5.1-10mm Export	T. O. Dahlstrand/Pres.
117. Walker Mfg. Co. Tenneco Co. Rt. 2 Newark Industrial Park #13 Hebron, OH 43025	Catalytic converters, pipes, mufflers	3714	512	Over 25mm Export over $50,000,000	John Novell/Personnel Richard DeMars/Pl. Mgr.
118. Wean United Inc. 1400 Grace Ave., NE Canton, OH 44705	Ironroll foundry	3322	250	10.1-25mm Rsch. facilities Export	R. J. Wean III/Pres. Edward Bauer/Pl. Mgr.

Note: (*) Respondants to the survey.

104

APPENDIX 6.3   Chi-Square and Gamma Statistics

Chi Square (χ^2) Test Statistics

Consider the following 2 x 2 table.

	A_1	A_2	
B_1	n_{11}	n_{12}	$n_{1.} = n_{11} + n_{12}$
B_2	n_{21}	n_{22}	$n_{2.} = n_{21} + n_{22}$

$n_{.1} = n_{11} + n_{21}$ $n_{.2} = n_{12} + n_{22}$ $N = n_{11} + n_{12} + n_{21} + n_{22}$

We are interested in determining whether the numbers of observations in the cells could have occurred by chance. To operationalize the idea of chance, we note that two events are considered statistically independent if the probability of their joint event is the simple product of the probability of each event. In the table, n_{11} is the observed frequency of the joint event ($A_1\ B_1$). The expected frequency, n_{11}, is the product of the probability of the joint event $P(A_1\ B_1)$, and N, the total number of observations. In general we do not know $P(A_1\ B_1)$. However, under the assumption that the frequencies in the table could have occurred by chance, we can calculate it by the definition of statistical independence:

$$P(A_1\ B_1) = P(A_1)\ P(B_1)$$

We can estimate the marginal probabilities, $P(A_1)$ and $P(B_1)$, by using the marginal proportions in the table:

and

$$P(A_1) = \frac{n_{11} + n_{21}}{N} = \frac{n_{.1}}{N}$$

$$P(B_1) = \frac{n_{11} + n_{12}}{N} = \frac{n_{1.}}{N}$$

Combining these results yields an estimate of the joint probability

$$\hat{P}(A_1 B_1) = \frac{n_{.1}\, n_{1.}}{N^2}$$

and an estimate of the expected cell frequency under the chance assumption

$$\hat{n}_{11} = \frac{n_{.1}\, n_{1.}}{N}$$

Given the actual and expected frequencies in a table, we need a criterion to determine whether the actual departures from the expected frequenceis are "large enough" for us to make the statement "The observed frequencies could not have occurred by chance." Two important comments are in order. First, we always expect some discrepancy between observed and expected; second, we never make statements like the one above with certainty. Instead, we attach a level of confidence to such a statement.

The chi square (χ^2) statistic is the most commonly used criterion for deciding whether observed frequencies are chance occurrences. It is computed according to the following formula:

$$\chi^2 = \sum_{i=1}^{R} \sum_{j=1}^{C} \frac{(n_{ij} - \hat{n}_{ij})^2}{\hat{n}_{ij}}$$

The notation used to describe the simple 2 x 2 table has been generalized to cover a table of R rows and C columns.

The χ^2 statistic has a probability distribution associated with it. It is a one-parameter distribution characterized by degrees of freedom. In this situation, degree of freedom is given by the formula

$$d.o.f = (R - 1)(C - 1).$$

Thus, the simple 2 x 2 table has one degree of freedom. It was mentioned above that we always expect observed and expected frequencies to differ to some degree, and thus we expect the χ^2 statistic to be greater than zero. How much more is given by the degrees of freedom. On average, a

χ^2 statistic computed on a table of frequencies generated by chance will equal its degree of freedom.

The decision problem is: How large should the χ^2 statistic be before we reject the hypothesis that the observed pattern was generated by chance? This answer is found by examining the probability distribution for the χ^2 statistic.

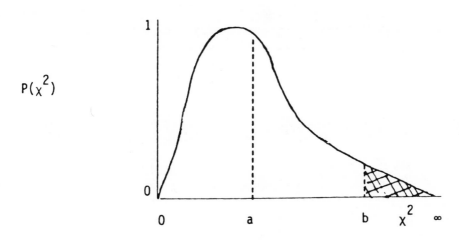

This figure represents a typical χ^2 probability distribution. The vertical axis is the probability associated with each value of the statistic on the horizontal axis. As with all probability distributions, the area under the curve equals 1. The dotted line a represents the expected value of χ^2 for this distribution, the degree of freedom. The dotted line at b is the critical value of the χ^2 statistic. This critical value is chosen so that the area under the curve to the right of b equals some small probability, usually .01 or .05. This critical value of the χ^2 statistic is used and interpreted in the following manner.

If the computed value of χ^2 given by the above formula is greater than the critical value given by a χ^2 probability distribution, the probability of an event's occurring by chance is very small—less than the probability represented by the crosshatched area in the figure. Furthermore, if the observed frequencies do not occur by chance, we conclude that some relationship between the two variables in the table generated the observed frequencies. The converse of the statement "The observed frequencies could have occurred by chance with less than 5 percent probability" is "We are 95 percent confident that a relationship exists between the two variables in the table."

This last interpretation is most common in interpreting tables with the χ^2 statistic.

Below is a set of critical values for a range of degrees of freedom that are defined by the 95 percent confidence level.

Degrees of Freedom	Critical Values
1	3.84
2	5.99
3	7.82
4	9.49
5	11.07
10	18.31
15	24.00
20	31.41
25	37.65
30	43.77

Gamma Coefficient

The gamma coefficient is used to measure the degree of association between two ordinal variables. Ordinal variables take on values that can be ordered by some criterion. Examples are high, medium, low, no difficulty, some difficulty, a great deal of difficulty.

The gamma coefficient describes the degree to which the ordered values on two variables align themslves across all the observations. Alignments can be positive (high with high, medium with medium, low with low) or negative (high with low, medium with medium, low with high). The value of gamma ranges from -1, perfect negative ordinal relation, through 0, no ordinal relation, to +1, perfect positive ordinal relation.

The formulas for computing gamma are too complex to provide intuitive understanding. Instead, consider the following 3 x 3 table.

	Low	Medium	High	
Low	6	2	0	8
Medium	15	22	6	43
High	3	34	19	56
	24	58	25	107

The computed value of gamma for this table is .69.
  • This table represents a moderately strong ordinal
relation; only the high-medium cell, with 34 observations,
appears to depart from the expected ordered alignment of
high-high. If the frequencies had spread over the table
according to the marginal proportions, gamma would be near
zero. If the frequencies clustered more closely along the
diagonal, gamma would be near 1.

Pearson Correlation Coefficient

The Pearson correlation coefficient is the standard measure
of association between two variables that take on meaningful
numerical values. It varies from -1, a perfect negative
correlation, through 0, no correlation, to +1, a perfect
positive correlation.
  Intuitively, the correlation coefficient is best illustrated
by a scatter plot. Each point in a scatter plot represents
an observation on a pair of variables, x and y. The formula
for the correlation coefficient computed on $n(x_1, y_1)$
observation pairs is

$$r = \frac{\sum\limits_{i=1}^{n} (x_i - \bar{x})(y_i - \bar{y})}{\sqrt{\left[\sum\limits_{i=1}^{n}(x_i - \bar{x})^2\right]\left[\sum\limits_{i=1}^{n}(y_i - \bar{y})^2\right]}}$$

where x and y are the means of x and y:

$$\bar{x} = \frac{1}{n}\sum\limits_{i=1}^{n} x_i \ , \ \bar{y} = \frac{1}{n}\sum\limits_{i=1}^{n} y_i \ .$$

Appendix 6.4 Reliability Determination Using the Spearman-Brown Formula

Subject	Score (X)	X^2	Score (Y)	Y^2	XY
1	35	1225	30	900	1050
2	29	841	21	441	609
3	8	64	8	64	64
4	21	441	24	576	504
5	19	361	16	256	304
6	30	900	25	625	750
7	25	625	26	676	650
8	36	1296	28	784	1008
9	49	2401	39	1521	1911
10	26	676	23	529	598
11	29	841	26	676	754
12	39	1521	36	1296	1404
13	36	1296	31	961	1116
14	41	1681	28	784	1148
15	30	900	26	676	780
16	25	625	18	324	450
17	27	729	27	729	729
18	28	784	21	441	588
19	28	784	27	729	756
20	20	400	22	484	440
21	24	576	18	324	432
22	26	676	25	625	650
23	24	576	19	361	456
24	25	625	25	625	625
25	40	1600	27	729	1080
26	25	625	25	625	625
27	21	441	20	400	420
28	10	100	12	144	120
29	17	289	11	121	187
30	42	1764	29	841	1218
SUM	835	25663	713	18267	21426

(The Score (X) is the sum of the ODD NUMBERED ITEMS 1, 3, 5, 7, 9, 11, 13, 15, 17, 19, 21, 23, 25; the Score (Y) is the sum of the EVEN NUMBERED ITEMS 2, 4, 6, 8, 10, 12, 14, 16, 18, 20, 22, 24, 26.)

$$r_{hh} = r_{XY} = \frac{n\Sigma XY - \Sigma X \Sigma Y}{[\,n\Sigma X^2 - (\Sigma X)^2\,]^{\frac{1}{2}}\,[\,n\Sigma Y^2 - (\Sigma Y)^2\,]^{\frac{1}{2}}}$$

$$= \frac{(30)(21426) - (835)(713)}{[(30)(25663) - (835)^2]^{\frac{1}{2}}\,[(30)(18267) - (713)^2]^{\frac{1}{2}}} = 0.884$$

$$\therefore\ r_{Rel.} = \frac{2r_{hh}}{1 + r_{hh}} = \frac{(2)(.884)}{1 + .884} = 0.938 \approx 0.94$$

111

7

The Research Results and Statistical Analyses

THE RESEARCH RESULTS: AN OVERVIEW

This chapter consists of two parts; the first explains how the research was done and the characteristics of the respondents. The second focuses on research results and statistical analyses. The statistical analyses will be compared with the results of the researcher's interviews with the licensees' executives. The goal is to see whether the statistical analyses are consistent with what is practiced in real life.

After the research instrument proved to be very reliable, with a strong correlation coefficient ($r^2 = .94$) in the pilot study, the questionnaire was mailed to all 118 firms. After one month, a second questionnaire was sent to nonrespondents. Following the second mailing, most of the nonrespondents were contacted by telephone. The goal was to entice the executives to participate in the survey and to make arrangements for the post-survey interviews with the executives. The goal was to get a firsthand feel for licensing activities as well as to substantiate the statistical analyses. A total of 51 complete and useful questionnaires were used in the statistical analyses (this is a 43 percent response rate).

Most of the information in the questionnaire was checked later with the public sources (such as Standard & Poor and Harris Ohio), as well as with the executives interviewed and the firms' annual reports. The aim was to make sure that the data used in the statistical analyses were reliable. Fortunately, most of the respondents were either the president, the vice-president, or one of the

112

other executives. The post-survey interviews with ten licensees' executives were with presidents or chief decision makers in international licensing area. Table 7.1 shows some characteristics of the companies surveyed.

TABLE 7.1 Characteristics of Ohio Licensees Surveyed

Size Group	No. of Employees	Annual Sales ($ mill)	Total	Respondents No.	Respondents Percent	Non-Respondents No.	Non-Respondents Percent
Small	1-99	25	50	24	47	26	39
Medium	100-499	100	38	13	25.5	25	37.2
Large	500+	100+	30	14	27.5	16	23.8
			118	51	100	67	100

Source: Based on original material compiled by the author.

Knowledge of international markets is perhaps the most important element in the internationalization of business. Without such knowledge, a domestic firm is unaware of international opportunities. Of the corporations surveyed, 84 percent indicated that they had international exposure prior to entering the licensing agreement. This exposure ranged from a foreign distribution agent (41 percent) to a full overseas manufacturing, sales, and service facility (27 percent). Table 7.2 shows the international interests of the companies surveyed.

Different firms used different methods to tap international opportunities. These methods could be classified into five categories. The first is the executives' personal contacts. Because of their experience and exposure to international markets, and because of the nature of their jobs, it is natural for them to have contacts overseas. This method ranked the highest in the survey (weighted average response of 42.8). The second category is direct marketing by the parties involved. This could be initiated by the licensee or by the licensor. Direct marketing ranked second and third in the survey. The third category is trade and scientific publications (*Tech Trade, Le Nouvelle*, etc.), associations (such as the L.E.S.), or

TABLE 7.2 Licensees' International Interests

	Number of Respondents	Percentage
Overseas manufacturing, sales, and service facilities	14	27
Overseas sales and service	8	16
Foreign distribution agents	21	41
Domestic operations	8	16
Total	51	100

Source: Based on original material compiled by the author.

conventions, which ranked fourth in the survey. The fourth method used by licensees to tap international markets and/or locate their licensors was licensing brokers. These brokers specialize in matching potential licensors and licensees. The last method is getting governmental or international institutional assistance. The government could be the home or the host government, and the international institution could be the United Nations, UNIDO, or WIPO.

Table 7.3 summarizes the methods used by licensees in this survey and the importance of each method as viewed by respondents to the survey.

TABLE 7.3 Methods Used by Licensees in Locating Technology

	Average Mean Response
Personal Contact	42.8
Direct marketing effort by licensee	33.8
Direct marketing effort by licensor	30.6
Trade & scientific publication, associations, and/or conventions	26.4
Foreign government and/or international institutions	14.6
Licensing brokers	14.6
Home government assistance	13.6

Source: Based on original material compiled by the author.

West Germany, the United Kingdom, and Japan accounted for more than 61 percent of the licensors in this survey, with West Germany leading the list (34 percent).

Table 7.4 shows relationship between the licensees and their licensors prior to the license agreement.

TABLE 7.4 Licensee-Licensor Relationship Before License

	Number of Respondents	Percentage
No relationship	26	51
Licensee as licensor's distribution agent	8	15
Licensor as licensee's distribution agent	4	8
Other licensing arrangement	6	12
Other (e.g., partnership)	7	14
Total	51	100

Source: Based on original material compiled by the author.

Most of the respondents to the survey were in nonelectrical manufacturing (SIC 35), chemicals (SIC 28), fabricated metal (SIC 34), and stone, clay, and glass (SIC 32).

Licensees indicated that they entered licensing agreements for various motives, including need for the technology, supplementing their own R&D, diversification, avoiding risks of R&D expenditure, or acquiring the right to operate because of patent laws. These licensees had realized that in order to survive the international competition, they had to have new and more efficient product(s) and/or process(es). There are two ways to stay competitive: (1) do your own internal R&D and develop new products or processes or (2) buy technology from external sources through licensing. Each option has its own advantages and disadvantages (see Chapter 3). The major advantages of developing one's own technology are independence and internationalization. The major disadvantages are the costs, the timing, and the NIH syndrome, which could alienate licensees' core-skilled employees (see Chapter 3).

The major advantages of licensing are the costs, timing, and risks. In most cases, the licensor has already introduced the technology in the home market, and therefore the product is commercially proven. The R&D costs are at least partially recovered. Thus the licensor, looking at the royalties as a residual income, can afford to sell the technology at a cost below what it would have cost the licensees had they decided to develop the product on their own. Since the product is commercially tested, the risks are minimal and, in most cases, the royalty payments are related to the volume of licensees' sales or profits. Also, the costs to the licensee are contingent upon the success of the licensed product. A major disadvantage of licensing technology, from the licensees' viewpoint, is the important issue of dependence on the licensor (see Chapter 5).

TABLE 7.5 Licensees' Motivation for Technology Licensing

	Weighted Average Response
To acquire the needed technology and/or supplement own R&D	38.2
To diversify operations	36.4
To avoid risk of R&D expenditure and/or to acquire technology not available in the U.S.	32.2
To acquire the right to operate because of patent	26.0

Source: Based on original material compiled by the author.

TESTING OF HYPOTHESES AND STATISTICAL ANALYSIS OF RESULTS

In this section the research hypotheses will be tested by using the test statistics explained in Chapter 6. Statistical analyses and interpretations will follow the tests for each hypothesis.

Hypothesis 1

H_0 In international technology licensing, the stages of the PLC and the licensee's size are independent.

H_1 Small-to-medium-sized licensees will tend to have had products that were in the declining stage of their PLC prior to licensing. (Table 7.6 summarizes the empirical results.)

TABLE 7.6 Licensees' Size and PLC

| | Product Life Cycle Stage | | |
Licensees' Size	Earlier	Later	Total
Small & medium	10 (27.03)	27 (72.97)	37
Large	9 (64.29)	5 (35.71)	14
Total	19	32	51

Note: Numbers in parentheses are row percentages.
SAS: Statistics for two-way tables.
Chi-square (χ^2) = 6.032; d.f. = 1; probability = .0140.
Continuity adj. χ^2 = 4.543; d.f. = 1; probability = .03
Gamma = -0.659.
Source: Based on original material compiled by the author.

Because χ^2 = 6.032 and the probability is .0140, the null hypothesis will be rejected. This implies that small-to-medium-sized licensees have had products that were at the declining stage of the PLC. As was explained earlier, in order for these firms (usually single-product) to survive, they need products. They either have to do in-house R&D or they have to buy the technology. Licensing of technology turns out to be the option chosen by the companies surveyed. For the companies surveyed, licensing of technology was basically an extension of their lives, without which they would have had to close their doors. This point was repeated by the executives interviewed. Perhaps the following statement by the president of a medium-sized machine tool company best summarizes their view:

> . . . We bought technology to stay competitive and without the Germans' help, we couldn't have done it. . . . It is probably cheaper to do it that way than to develop it yourself. There's a limit to your capability, and I think we are seeing more and more of this. Not just companies our size, but even IBM and others. . . . Why does GM have a deal with Isuzu? or Toyota? Or why does AT&T have a deal with Olivetti?[1]

Hypothesis 2

H_0 Licensees' size and type of licensed technology are independent.

H_1 Small-to-medium-sized licensees are more likely to acquire licenses to manufacture product(s) whose manufacturing process (know-how) is related to that of their existing products (same product line, same process, or same SIC) than are larger licensees.

TABLE 7.7 Licensees' Size and Type of Licensed Technology

| Licensees' Size | Type of Licensed Technology | | Total |
	Related Tech.	Unrelated Tech.	
Small & medium	27 (72.97)	10 (27.03)	37
Large	5 (35.71)	9 (64.29)	14
Total	32	19	51

Note: Numbers in parentheses are row percentages.
SAS: Statistics for two-way tables.
Chi-square (χ^2) = 6.032; d.f. = 1; probability = .014.
Continuity adj. χ^2 = 4.543; d.f. = 1; probability = .033.
Gamma = .659.
Source: Based on original material compiled by the author.

Because of their limited resources and expertise, and because of easier technology diffusion, small-to-medium-sized licensees tend to buy technology directly related to their existing technology (same product line, same process, and so on). They normally lack the required resources (R&D) to develop technology that they need. In most cases, they buy the related technology in order to survive; if they want to buy unrelated technology, they must have a reasonable number of qualified scientists and engineers to facilitate the transfer. If they can afford to have such core-skill personnel, perhaps they can afford to live without foreign technology. But the major problem is that these firms usually lack such personnel. As a result, they have to stay with what they know best and what they do best.

Almost 73 percent of small and medium-sized licensees surveyed indicated that they bought similar and related technology. But 65 percent of the larger licensees bought unrelated technology, which clearly indicates that larger firms can afford to venture into new fields because of their resources. A χ^2 of 6.032 with a probability of .014 indicates that the test statistic is significant at .01 and the null hypothesis is rejected. A gamma of .659 shows a moderately strong association between the variables (licensee size and type of technology acquired).

Interviews with the licensees' executives substantiated the above findings. The consensus among the executives can be expressed as follows:

> . . . Similar products require the least amount of investment and changes on our part. We already had the resources and knowledge to accommodate the technology. . . . The transfer process was easier and faster . . . that's what we wanted. We couldn't afford spending more on R&D and/or hiring new personnel. . . . Different or unrelated product(s) is a whole new world to us. It is like starting from scratch and we couldn't afford that.

More than 64 percent of those surveyed indicated that the technology they bought was similar to their own technology (product) or used a similar manufacturing process. Hypothesis 2 statistically verifies that small-to-medium-sized licensees acquire a technology similar to their own.

More than 60 percent of the respondents indicated that the licensed products were in the later stages of the PLC. Only 39 percent bought technology in its earlier stages. Interviews with the executives revealed that almost all of those who bought technology at an earlier stage (R&D level or early commercial use) either had the qualified core-skill personnel (more than 3.5 percent of sales spent on R&D or more than 25 core-skilled personnel for every 1,000 employees), or licensing was more of a marriage of convenience for both parties. The bottom line is that it is almost impossible to buy technology at its earlier stages (especially at the R&D stage) without sufficient numbers of qualified scientists or engineers on your payroll. Such an attempt is doomed to failure. Hypothesis 3 statistically substantiates this point, and Table 7.8 summarizes the licensed products' PLC stages in the licensors' market.

TABLE 7.8 Licensed Product's PLC Stage in Licensors' Market

Stage of PLC	Number of Respondents	Percentage of Respondents	Rank
R&D	3	5.8	3
Early commercial (less than 5 years)	17	33.4	2
Mature (in commercial use more than five years)	28	55.0	1
Declining	3	5.8	3
Total	51	100.0	

Source: Based on original material compiled by the author.

Hypothesis 3

H_0 Licensees' R&D and technical capabilities (core skills) and the PLC stage of the technology acquired are independent.

H_1 Licensees with a high ratio of scientists and engineers are more likely to acquire a license at an earlier stage in the IPLC than are those with fewer core-skilled employees.

The null hypothesis will be rejected because $\chi^2 = 4.073$, degree of freedom = 1, and probability = .0436 (significance level). The alternative hypothesis will be accepted, which is what was expected. When a product (technology) is in the earlier stages of IPLC, the degree of uncertainty about the product is higher because little is known about it and its commercial success. At earlier stages (R&D, introduction, or growth), the recipient of technology (licensee) must have the resources (scientists and engineers) to understand the technology and to implement it. Licensees with a higher percentage of their employees as R&D or technical can afford to enter a licensing agreement for a product in the earlier stages of the IPLC.

In the sample, 56.5 percent of licensees with core-skill personnel bought technology in its earlier stage, but only 28.6 percent of those without core skills could afford to take the risk of entering a license agreement for a product at an earlier stage. Of the respondents, 71 percent indicated that they bought technology when it was commercially proven or in its later stages of the IPLC (see Table 7.9).

TABLE 7.9 Licensees' Characteristics and PLC

	PLC of Licensed Technology		
Characteristics	Earlier Stage	Later Stage	Total
With core skills	13 (56.52)	10 (43.48)	23
Without core skills	8 (28.57)	20 (71.43)	28
Total	21	30	51

Note: Numbers in parentheses are row percentages.
SAS: Statistics for two-way tables.
Chi-square (χ^2) = 4.073; d.f. = 1; probability = .0436.
Phi = .283.
Continuity adj. χ^2 = 3.001; d.f. = 1; probability = .08.
Gamma = .529.
Source: Based on original material compiled by the author.

Hypothesis 4

H_0 Licensees' R&D and technical capabilities (core-skills) and technical uncertainties associated with the licensed technology, are independent.

H_1 Licensees with a high ratio of core skills (technically competent) will tend to begin operations under license in environments of higher technical uncertainty than those with a lower proportion or no such personnel.

Because χ^2 = 5.059 with one degree of freedom and probability of .245 (significance level), as well as continuity-adjusted χ^2 of 5.318, one degree of freedom, and probability of .0458, the null hypothesis will be rejected at the .05 level.

TABLE 7.10 Licensees' Characteristics, by Degree of Technical Uncertainty

Licensees' Characteristics	Technical Uncertainty		Total
	Low	High	
With core skills	8 (34.78)	15 (65.22)	23
Without core skills	18 (66.67)	9 (33.33)	27
Total	26	24	50

Note: Numbers in parentheses are row percentages.
SAS: Statistics for two-way tables.
Chi-square (χ^2) = 5.059; d.f. = 1; probability = .245.
Continuity adj. χ^2 = 5.318; d.f. = 1; probability = .0458.
Gamma = -.579.
Source: Based on original material compiled by the author.

A gamma of -.579 shows a moderate inverse association between research variables (licensees' characteristics and degree of technical uncertainty associated with the licensed technology). The alternative hypothesis will, therefore, be accepted.

The empirical results are consistent with the alternative hypothesis. Of the licensees with core skills, 65.2 percent acquired technology with high uncertainty. On the other hand, almost two-thirds of those without core skills purchased technology with a low degree of uncertainty.

The PLC and technical uncertainties are closely related. At the introduction stage, technical uncertainties are much higher than in the standardized stage. Naturally, licensees without core-skills personnel cannot afford to acquire technology in its earlier stages. They do not have the technical expertise to comprehend the technology. This is not the case for licensees with core skills. Their core-skill employees allow them to venture into new technology, and the diffusion process is smoother.

Both Vernon and Hirsch have emphasized the lack of product standardization and fluctuations in required materials and processes as the major sources for higher technical uncertainties in the earlier stages of PLC.

The product itself may be quite unstandardized for a time, its inputs, its processing and its final specifications may cover a wide range. Contrast the great variety of automobiles produced and marketed before 1910 with the thoroughly stand-ardized products of the 1930's.[2]

As a product goes through different stages of its life cycle, technical uncertainty declines. At the introduction stage, techniques change very rapidly; in the growth stage, variations in techniques still are frequent; and in the mature stage, changes and innovations are very few. The technical uncertainty declines over time and with the maturity of the product. It also varies from product to product.

Technical uncertainty varies from product to prod-uct, even at the same stage of the product life cycle. That is, there will likely be more technical uncertainty in the early stage of a new video tape recorder than the early stage of a new pair of shoes, although in both cases this uncertainty will decline over time.[3]

Hypothesis 5

H_0 Licensees' R&D core skills and marketing uncer-tainties associated with the licensed technology are independent.

H_1 Licensees with a high ratio of core-skills employees will tend to begin operations under license in environments of higher marketing uncertainty than those with a lower proportion or no such personnel.

Because continuity-adjusted χ^2 = 9.617, degree of freedom = 1, and probability = .0019, the null hypothesis will be rejected. The alternative hypothesis, which basical-ly says that licensees with core skills will tend to acquire licenses to manufacture where the degree of marketing uncertainty is high, will be accepted.

There is also a direct relationship between marketing uncertainties and the IPLC. The newer the technology in international markets, the higher the marketing uncer-tainties. Licensees with qualified core skills (technical and marketing) can better evaluate the new technology and its chances of success in international markets. This does not imply that when a product is a success in one market, it

TABLE 7.11 Licensees' Characteristics, by Degree of Marketing Uncertainty

Licensees' Characteristics	Marketing Uncertainty		
	Low	High	Total
With core skills	6 (26.09)	17 (73.91)	23
Without core skills	20 (74.07)	7 (25.93)	27
Total	26	24	50

Note: Numbers in parentheses are row percentages.
SAS: Statistics for two-way tables.
Chi-square (χ^2) = 11.458; d.f. = 1; probability = .0007.
Continuity adj. χ^2 = 9.617; d.f. = 1; probability = .0019.
Gamma = 0.780.
Source: Based on original material compiled by the author.

will be a success in international markets. Cases are numerous where a product has been a success (technically and/or in terms of marketing) in one market and a failure in other markets due to technical and/or marketing mix. A prime example of a technical failure-turned-success is the case of Honda. When it introduced its cars in the United States in the mid-1960s its subcompact vehicles were not designed for U.S. highways. Obviously the car had to be withdrawn from the market. A few years later, Honda introduced a different version of the Civic, which is among the most popular subcompact cars in the United States.

A prime example of marketing failure is the Chevy Nova in Spanish-speaking countries. Regardless of its technical performance in the United States and around the world, Nova did not have much success in those nations. "No va" means "no go" in Spanish. Apparently customers in Spanish-speaking countries did not want to buy something that wouldn't move. They wanted a reliable means of transportation.

The analogy can be made between declining marketing uncertainty and the diffusion process involved in the adopting of a new product. Adopters of any innovation are generally classified into five groups, according to the order in which they adopt the innovation.[4]

Innovators	first	2.5%
Early adopters	next	13.5%
Early majority	next	34%
Late majority	next	34%
Laggards	remaining	16%

Innovators tend to be venturesome and highly knowledgeable about international markets. In some cases they deviate from the norm. Early adopters tend to have a higher position in society and in most cases are opinion leaders. They have some knowledge of the product or innovation. Those in the early majority tend to rush to adopt the innovation or product as soon as they are convinced that opinion leaders have done so. The late majority is usually skeptical and tends to wait until public opinion strongly favors the innovation. Laggards tend to be older, to be suspicious of innovations, and to take the past and tradition as their point of reference. Basically, the adoption process is conceived of as a set of five mental stages through which an individual passes, from first hearing about an innovation until he or she adopts it: (1) awareness, (2) interest, (3) evaluation, (4) trial, and (5) adoption.[5]

Licenses with core skills (early adopters and early majority), after having heard about the technology and become interested in it, are capable of evaluating the technology or adopting it. These licensees can buy technology at a level where the product or process is not commercially proven. They have the ability to develop and commercialize the product.

Licensees without core skills, like the late majority and laggards, wait until public opinion strongly favors adoption of a technology. They don't have the resources to evaluate it. They have to wait for it to be commercially proven, and usually purchase the technology at production level where there are no or minimal technical or marketing uncertainties.

A licensee is considered to be a dominant when it is larger than its licensor in terms of total sales, number of employees, and/or R&D expenditure. In this survey, most U.S. licensees were nondominant. They were smaller than their foreign licensors in terms of sales (68 percent), number of employees (66 percent), and R&D expenditure (68 percent). When a licensee is larger than its licensor, it will have the upper hand in the negotiation process and probably can negotiate a license agreement in its favor.

This dominance provides the licensee with the opportunity to negotiate a license agreement with a lower royalty payment for the licensed technology than a nondominant licensee could obtain. A dominant licensee will be able to enter an agreement with fewer restrictions (for instance, on export, procurement).

TABLE 7.12 Size Comparison of Licensors and Licensees

	Sales		Employees		R&D Expenditure	
	No.	%	No.	%	No.	%
Licensee smaller than licensor	34	68	33	66	34	68
Licensee equal to licensor	1	2	4	8	5	10
Licensee larger than licensor	15	30	13	26	11	22
Total	50	100	50	100	50	100

Source: Based on original material compiled by the author.

Table 7.12 compares the licensees in the sample with their licensors in terms of total sales, number of employees, and R&D expenditure. Hypothesis 6 is a direct attempt to verify the above arguments. It focuses on the royalty payment and restrictions in the license agreement, and tests the independence between royalty rate and restrictions of the licensees.

The royalty rate and number of restrictions in the license agreement reinforce the idea that the dominant characteristics of the licensee play an important role in the compensation arrangements and the number of restrictions in the license agreement.

The compensation arrangement can take different forms. A percentage of sales or volume is the most widely used method (49.4 percent). Minimum annual payments and lump-sum payments are the two next important methods in this research (18.8 percent and 16.5 percent, respectively). Table 7.13 summarizes the types of compensation arrangements and their frequency of use by U.S. licensees.

TABLE 7.13 International Technology Licensing: Types of Compensation Arrangements

Type of Compensation	Number	Percentage
Percentage of sales or volume	42	49.4
Minimum annual payment	16	18.8
Lump-sum payment	14	16.5
Licensed product(s)	8	9.4
Graduated decreasing royalty	4	4.7
Graduated increasing royalty	1	1.2
Total	85	100.0

Source: Based on original material compiled by the author.

Hypothesis 6

H_0 The dominant characteristics of licensees and the royalty rate are independent.

H_1 Dominant licensees (larger than licensor in terms of size and/or R&D expenditure) are more likely to be able to negotiate a lower royalty rate than are nondominant licensees.

Because $\chi^2 = 6.38$ with one degree of freedom, the null hypothesis will be rejected and the alternative hypothesis will be accepted at the .021 significance level. This indicates that dominant licensees in the sample actually paid a lower rate than nondominant ones. Eighty-three percent of the dominant licensees were able to negotiate a license agreement with a royalty of 3 percent or lower, and 16.7 percent had to pay more than 3 percent. A gamma of .7 indicates a strong association between the research variables (dominant characteristics and royalty rate).

On the other hand, the case for nondominant licensees was quite different. They were divided almost in half: 53 percent were paying more than 3 percent of their net sales of the licensed technology to their licensors. Almost 47 percent were paying 3 percent or less. This raised the

TABLE 7.14 Licensees' Characteristics by Royalty Payments

	Royalty as a Percentage of Net Sales		
	Less Than 3%	More Than 3%	Total
Dominant	15 (83.33)	3 (16.67)	18
Nondominant	15 (46.88)	17 (53.13)	32
Total	30	20	50

Note: Numbers in parentheses are row percentages.
SAS: Statistics for two-way tables.
Chi-square (χ^2) = 6.38; d.f. = 1; probability = .0115.
Continuity adj. χ^2 = 4.952; d.f. = 1; probability = .0261.
Gamma = .700.
Source: Based on original material compiled by the author.

question of how these licensees managed to negotiate such low rates. Further investigation and interviews with the licensees' executives revealed that most (72 percent) of these licensees were able to negotiate a lower rate because their licensors were more interested in things other than royalty payments. The licensors in most cases were more interested in establishing their product in the U.S. market and/or lacked the resources to exploit the U.S. market on their own (see the Masstron Scales case).

Another reason for such an arrangement was cross-licensing arrangements between the licensors and the licensees. The licensors apparently had sacrificed royalty rates for access to new developments in the area of technology licensed by their licensees. In other cases the competition in the licensors' market and the type of licensed technology had a major impact on the royalty rate. The number of restrictions imposed on the licensee was also important in the compensation arrangements. The higher the number of restrictions, the lower the royalty rate.

In the following paragraphs the empirical research on the pricing of technology licensing by other scholars will be reviewed.

The empirical results on pricing of technology licensing

and royalty rates are inconclusive and vary within a wide range, depending on the nature of the industry and the type of licensing agreement.[6] Goldscheider and Marshall found that the royalty rate for all industries was 5–6 percent of the licensee's net sales.[7] Enlow found the royalty rate to be 3–5 percent in the computer field.[8] Conte studies royalty payments in the pharmaceutical industry and concluded that the rate was 10–15 percent of the licensee's net sales for exclusive licenses. The rate for a sole license was found to be 7–10 percent, and for a nonexclusive agreement the rate was 4–7 percent of the licensee's net sales.[9] Eckstrom found that the royalty rate for petroleum processes and products was around 1 percent of net sales (Union Oil Company) and in some cases as low as .10 percent, but his conclusion was that the overall rate for the petroleum industry was about 5 percent of net sales.[10] Hashbarger found the rate in the chemical industry to be 3–5 percent of the licensee's net sales.[11] Talbott put the royalty rate for the automobile industry at 1–5 percent.[12] Coogan concluded that the royalty rate for an exclusive license in the wood and paper products industry was 6 percent, and for a nonexclusive license was 4–5 percent.[13] Orleans examined the pricing of the licensing of technology for "high tech," such as applied physics, optics, and electronics; the royalty rate was found to be about 5 percent of the licensee's net sales.[14]

Hypothesis 6(b)

H_0 Licensees' dominant characteristics and the number of restrictions in the license agreement are independent.

H_1 Dominant licensees are more likely to be able to negotiate fewer restrictions in the license agreement than are nondominant ones.

Because χ^2 is 6.63 and the degree of freedom is 1, the null hypothesis will be rejected at the .01 significance level. As a result, the alternative hypothesis will be accepted. The gamma of .68 indicates a strong association between dominance and number of restrictions in the license agreements. In fact, 76.5 percent of the dominant licensees were able to negotiate license agreements with one or no restrictions. The case for nondominant licensees is different. Almost 62 percent of the nondominant licensees had to accept two or more restrictions in their license agreements. This is consistent with the earlier discussion

TABLE 7.15 Licensees' Dominance, by Number of Restrictions in License Agreement

	Number of Restrictions		
	One or Less	Two or More	Total
Dominant	13 (76.47)	4 (23.53)	17
Nondominant	13 (38.24)	21 (61.76)	34
Total	26	25	51

Note: Numbers in parentheses are row percentages.
SAS: Statistics for two-way tables.
Chi-square (χ^2) = 6.63; d.f. = 1; probability = .01.
Continuity adj. χ^2 = 5.188; d.f. = 1; probability = .0227.
Gamma = .680.
Source: Based on original material compiled by the author.

of licensees' dominance and their bargaining power in the licensing negotiations. The restrictions are of various types, with geographical limits the most widely used.

This research does not deal with the legal aspects of some of these restrictions, particularly the geographical (for instance on export) and procurement ones. It is illegal (a violation of antitrust laws) to impose such restrictions (typing clauses) on the licensee. Analysis and implications of such restrictive clauses are not central to this study.

In order to use technology licensing as a strategy for market penetration (as a licensor) and for tapping international sources of technology (as a licensee), firms need what Welch calls "the licensing package."[15] The main components of the licensing package are essentially technical in nature, and include patent and know-how (technical, managerial, and/or marketing).

Nonpatentable know-how is generally considered by users to be the critical part of technology transfers. Frequently the technological knowledge incorporated in patents is of limited value to potential users because of additional work needed prior to the introduction of the product in the market. Increasingly, sellers and buyers of technology recognize the value of commercial know-how in various forms. In many cases, the commercial accompaniment is the preeminent motivation for the licensee's seeking the technology. [16]

In view of the importance of the commercial know-how, it should be natural for the licensees in this survey to prefer the patent-plus-technical assistance package over pure patent rights. Table 7.16 shows the components of the licensing agreement.

TABLE 7.16 Components of License Agreements

	Number of Respondents	Percentage
Patent rights only	11	21.2
Patent rights plus technical assistance (know-how)	36	71.0
Other	4	7.8
Total	51	100.0

Source: Based on original material compiled by the author.

EMPIRICAL TEST OF THE LCM

Hypothesis 7 is a direct attempt to test the LCM empirically. As was explained in Chapter 5, licensees who have completed the licensing cycle (stage 4 of the LCM) have a tendency to cancel their licensing agreements. In general, cancellation of the license agreement may result from (1) expiration of the patent, (2) disagreement over marketing and/or compensation arrangements, (3) obsolescence or noncompetitiveness of the licensed technology, (4) licensee's technical competence.

Sixty-four percent of the respondents to the survey indicated that they had completed the licensing cycle and had canceled their licensing agreements. Table 7.17 summarizes these licensees' reasons for canceling their license agreements. Seventy-two percent of the cancellations were because of licensees' technical competence, technology

TABLE 7.17 Licensees' Reasons for License Agreement Cancellation

	Number	Percentage
Patent expiration	9	27.3
Disagreement on marketing and/or compensation arrangements	7	21.2
Obsolete or noncompetitive technology	7	21.2
Licensee's competence	10	30.3
Total	33	100.0

Source: Based on original material compiled by the author.

obsolescence, or disagreement over marketing and/or compensation arrangements. Fifty-eight percent of these licensees had continuous licensing agreements, and 42 percent had one-time agreements (see Table 7.18).

Hypothesis 7 will be statistically tested in three separate but interrelated ways: (1) licensee's reasons for canceling the agreement, (2) licensee's R&D capabilities, and (3) licensee's dependence on the licensor and/or production difficulties.

Hypothesis 7(a)

H_0 Licensing cycle and type of licensing agreement are independent.

H_1 Licensees with continuous license agreements are more likely to go through the licensing cycle than are those with one-time agreements.

Because χ^2 is 8.812, with one degree of freedom and probability of .003 (significance level), the null hypothesis will be rejected and the alternative will be accepted. A gamma of -.822 shows a very strong inverse association between type of license agreement and licensee's reasons for canceling the license.

Seventy-three percent of licensees with continuous license agreements had canceled the agreement because of their competence, and 26 percent had canceled it because of the expiration of the patent life and/or disagreement with their licensors. On the other hand, 78.6 percent of licensees with a one-time agreement had canceled the agreement because of expiration of the patent and/or disagreement with licensors.

TABLE 7.18 License Agreement Type, by Licensee Cancellation Reasons

License Agreement Type	Patent Life/ Disagreement	Licensee's Competence	Total
Continuous	5 (26.32)	14 (73.68)	19
One-time	11 (78.57)	3 (21.43)	14
Total	16	17	33

Note: Numbers in parentheses are row percentages.
SAS: Statistics for two-way tables.
Chi-square (χ^2) = 8.812; d.f. = 1; probability = .003.
Continuity adj. χ^2 = 6.844; d.f. = 1; probability = .008.
Gamma = -.822.
Source: Based on original material compiled by the author.

LICENSE AGREEMENT TYPE AND LICENSEES' CHARACTERISTICS

Crookell classified licensing agreements into three major categories: [17]

1. All technology currently developed or to be developed by licensor
2. All licensor's technology now in place (the licensee must have in-house skills to develop future change itself)
3. License for a specific patented product, component, or process.

The first type is different from the second and third because it includes future technology to be developed by the licensor. This type of license agreement is basically continuous, while the second and third are one-time agreements. In this book, the licensing agreements are divided into two broad categories: (1) continuous, a lasting but renewable agreement between the parties; and (2) one-time, which includes a license for patent only or a license for patent plus technical know-how.

The patent without know-how may be of limited value to the licensee but, like other elements in the licensing package, it contributes to the marketability of the whole. For technology recipients, the existence of a patent is often the first item in their consideration of the technology or offer. It represents a stamp of technological credibility. A number of Australian firms, for example, have found that in order to reach the first stage of market penetration in the United States, it is necessary to be able to offer U.S. patent rights.[18]

The success of a one-time agreement including patent plus know-how (licensing package) depends on the technical and marketing capabilities of the licensee. Since the ultimate success of the licensing arrangement depends on the success of the licensee, the contribution of the licensor will have a great impact on the end result. Unless the licensee has the capabilities to absorb the technology and market it successfully, the one-time license will be doomed to failure. This doesn't mean that the licensee must have the core skills prior to the licensing agreement; but the licensee should realize that in order to absorb and apply the acquired technology, it needs to develop core skills with the assistance received through the licensing arrangement. This assistance can be both technical and marketing—in essence, what Welch calls commercial accompaniment.

The continuous license agreement includes a lasting, renewable relationship. Much depends on the ability of both parties to establish and nurture a productive, interactive relationship, for it is through effective relationships that the technology is successfully transferred.[19] If the licensee does not have the necessary core skills prior to a licensing agreement, and if it wants to achieve technological competence within a reasonable time, it must develop those core skills through the licensing process. Welch explains the licensing activities in what he calls the "licensing process." It includes pre- and post-agreement activities that will be critically important to both parties.

Hypothesis 7 deals with the types of licensing agreements and licensees' characteristics. Hypothesis 8 deals with the license type and the number of restrictions imposed on the licensee. Before getting into the discussion and empirical tests of those hypotheses, it is appropriate to see what type of licensing agreements the U.S. (Ohio) licensees have. Table 7.19 shows that almost 61 percent of the respondents to the survey had continuous licensing

TABLE 7.19 Types of Licensing Agreements

	Number of Respondents	Percentage
One-time technology transfer (current technology	20	39.2
Continuous technology transfer	31	60.8
Total	51	100.0

Source: Based on original material compiled by the author.

agreements, as opposed to 39 percent with a one-time agreement.

Hypothesis 7(b)

H_0 Licensees' R&D level and capabilities, and type of licensing agreement are independent.

H_1 Licensees with continuous technology agreements are more likely to develop their own in-house R&D competence than are those with one time agreements.

Because $\chi^2 = 10.679$ with one degree of freedom, the null hypothesis will be rejected at the .001 level and the alternative hypothesis will be accepted. A gamma of -.845 indicates a very strong inverse association between the license type (continuous or one-time) and licensees' R&D capabilities. Ninety-three percent of licensees with a continuous license indicated that their R&D capabilities have increased as a result of the license agreement. Only 30 percent of licensees with a one-time agreement were able to increase their R&D capabilities; 70 percent indicated that their R&D capabilities in fact decreased or remained unchanged. Post-survey interviews with licensees' executives revealed that the main reason was that the licensees didn't need as many R&D personnel after the agreement. Although they had bought technology on a one-time basis, the agreement in most cases was a complete licensing package in which the licensor provided technical and marketing know-how. As one senior executive put it:

TABLE 7.20 License Agreement Type, by Licensees' R&D Capabilities

	R&D Capabilities		
License Type	Decreased	Increased	Total
Continuous	2 (6.45)	29 (93.25)	31
One-time	14 (70.00)	6 (30.00)	20
Total	16	35	51

Note: Numbers in parentheses are row percentages.
SAS: Statistics for two-way tables.
Chi-square (χ^2) = 10.679; d.f. = 1; probability = .0011.
Continuity adj. χ^2 = 8.522; d.f. = 1; probability = .0011.
Gamma = -.845.
Source: Based on original material compiled by the author.

Immediately with the licensing arrangement, we realized that it was cheaper to buy the whole package and let them do the job [R&D]. All we needed was a few qualified engineers to adapt the technology. We had no reason to keep our R&D people and pay them very high [salaries], or at least [not] that many. . . . Our relationship with our licensor is a very close one and they have helped us very generously. . . . Ten years down the road if we need new technology, we would not hesitate to contact our present licensor. If they have it and if they are reasonable, we will buy it from them. Otherwise we get it from somewhere else. We will see more and more licensing arrangements in the future. The costs [R&D] are half overseas [compared with the United States].[20]

Hypothesis 7(c)

H_0 The type of license agreement and the level of production difficulty associated with the licensed technology and the degree of the licensee's dependence are independent.

H$_1$ Licensees with a continuous license agreement are more likely to be able to reduce or eliminate the production difficulties associated with the licensed technology and to reduce their dependence on the licensors than those with one-time agreements, provided they go through the LCM.

TABLE 7.21 License Agreement Type, by Degree of Production Difficulties

	Degree of Production Difficulties		
	Decreased	Increased	Total
Continuous	27 (87.1)	4 (12.9)	31
One-time	7 (35.0)	13 (65.0)	20
Total	34	17	51

Note: Numbers in parentheses are row percentages.
SAS: Statistics for two-way tables.
Chi-square (χ^2) = 8.4; d.f. = 1; probability = .0038.
Continuity adj. χ^2 = 6.641; d.f. = 1; probability = .001.
Gamma = .741.
Source: Based on original material compiled by the author.

Because χ^2 = 8.4 with one degree of freedom, the null hypothesis will be rejected at the .0038 significance level and the alternative hypothesis will be accepted. The gamma of .741 shows a strong association between license type and the degree of production difficulties associated with the licensed technology.

Eighty-seven percent of the licensees with a continuous agreement indicated that the degree of production difficulties associated with licensed technology decreased; only 13 percent indicated that it either remained unchanged or increased. Of licensees with a one-time arrangement, 65 percent had increased difficulty and 35 percent had decreased difficulty.

When the agreement is a continuous one, the relationship between the parties is closer, particularly if the licensee has core skills of its own. Because of the vested interest that the licensor has in the contract, the licensee's success is its ultimate goal in the licensing agreement. In most cases, the licensor is interested in a lasting and renewable relationship. The continuous license usually contains cross-licensing arrangements through which the licensor will have access to the developments of the licensed technology or, in some cases, the spillovers.

The licensee, however, must be cautious. A continuous licensing agreement is beneficial if the licensee realizes that it should not be at the mercy of the licensor. A licensee with technical competence not only understands the technology but absorbs and applies it better and faster. The licensing agreement and cooperation with the licensor do not need to end when and if the licensee achieves competence. Both parties could benefit from cross-licensing and no-royalty arrangements. They could be licensor as well as licensee, and could share the high costs of R&D. The important message is that the licensee should try to learn the art or technique of "fishing" if it does not want to be dependent on the licensor for the "fish." Table 7.22 summarizes the licensees' views of licensing impacts. The results empirically verify hypotheses 7b and 7c.

TABLE 7.22 Licensees' Views of Licensing Impacts

	Decreased		Unchanged		Increased	
	No.	%	No.	%	No.	%
Production difficulties	34	66.7	15	29.4	2	3.9
Licensee's profit margin	7	14.3	18	36.7	24	49.0
Licensee's R&D capabilities	4	7.8	12	23.5	35	68.7
Licensee's dependence on licensor	35	68.7	13	25.4	3	5.9

Source: Based on original material compiled by the author.

Hypothesis 8

H_0 Type of license agreement and number of restrictions in the agreement are independent.

H_1 License agreements on a continuous basis are more likely to have more restrictions (geographical, procurement) than noncontinuous or one-time agreements.

TABLE 7.23   License Agreement Type, by Number of Restrictions

| | Number of Restrictions | | |
	One or Less	Two or More	Total
Continuous	6 (19.35)	25 (80.65)	31
One-time	14 (70.00)	6 (30.00)	20
Total	20	31	51

Note: Numbers in parentheses are row percentages.
SAS: Statistics for two-way tables.
Chi-square (χ^2) = 13.081; d.f. = 1; probability = .0003.
Continuity adj. χ^2 = 11.043; d.f. = 1; probability = .0009.
Gamma = -.813.
Source: Based on original material compiled by the author.

Because χ^2 is 13.08 and the degree of freedom is 1, the null hypothesis will be rejected and the alternative hypothesis will be accepted. The gamma of -.813 shows a very strong inverse association between license type (continuous or one-time) and number of restrictions in the license agreement. This is because, with the continuous type, the licensee will have access to the new developments of the technology by the licensor.

The most important restrictions are (1) geographical, (2) procurement, (3) cross-licensing (grant-back).

The legal aspect of these restrictions is not central to this study. The important point is that when the licensee acquires a patent only (one-time), the patent may be of no great value. When the agreement is for the patent plus technical assistance (licensing package), the licensor not only provides the licensee with the legal rights but must facilitate the technology transfer (through its scientists and engineers). The adaptation process is not free of costs, and the licensee has to pay them. When the licensing agreement calls for a continuous transfer of technology from the licensor to the licensee, the transfer includes not only the current technology but the future development as well. Consequently, the costs associated with the continuous transfer (current and future) are going to be higher than those of a one-time transfer.

The licensee has to compensate the licensor for these costs.[21] In many cases, the compensation may take the form of restrictions in the license agreement. Geographical restrictions limit the licensee's operations to a specific market or region (for instance, North America). The procurement restriction is a kind of tying clause forcing the licensee to buy certain parts or materials from the licensor. Therefore, in addition to the licensing income, the licensor has the possibility of building up sales of associated plant and equipment, parts, and/or raw materials.

In a study of Finnish companies licensing to in-dependent foreign licensees, it was found that the aggregate value of exports of associated plant and inputs was more than double the value of licensing income (Oravainen, 1979, p. 99). Over one-third of respondent firms in an Australian study indicated that licensing has produced sales of associated product.[22]

Table 7.24 summarizes the types of restrictions in the license agreements and their importance to U.S. licensees responding to the survey.

TABLE 7.24 Types of Restrictions in the Licensing Agreement

	Number of Respondents	Percentage
Geographical	24	47.0
Procurement	6	11.8
Cross-licensing (grant-back)	18	35.3
Other	3	5.9
Total	51	100.0

Source: Based on original material compiled by the author.

Tables 7.25 and 7.26 summarize the statistical analyses. Table 7.25 focuses on the first six hypotheses, and Table 7.26 summarizes hypotheses 7 and 8.

ANALYSES OF THE RESEARCH HYPOTHESES
AND THE EMPIRICAL RESULTS

Summaries of the research hypotheses' expectations (ex-ante) are in Tables 5.1 and 5.2. Summaries of the empirical results (ex-post) are in Tables 7.25 and 7.26. A comparison of Tables 5.1 and 7.25 (related to the first six hypotheses) clearly indicate that the empirical results were consistent with the research hypotheses' expectations. The corresponding cells are numbered (that is, the number "H1, H2," and so on, appears in the center of four factors that make up the cell) for identification of each research hypothesis and empirical result.

The non-numbered cells are indirect implications of the research hypotheses. The empirical results are consistent with the expectation in all of the non-numbered cells except in two: (1) the licensee's size versus the royalty rate, and (2) the licensee's size (small and medium only) and the number of restrictions in the license agreement.

One reason for such inconsistency is that the royalty rate is more a function of the licensee's other characteristics, such as core skills and dominance (for instance, R&D spending) than of its size. Hypothesis 6 directly tests the independence of the licensee's dominance from the royalty rate, and the empirical results are very consistent with the research hypothesis. A closer look at the licensee's core skills in relation to the royalty rate substantiates this argument.

The relative measure of the licensee's characteristics (for instance, the licensee's R&D spending compared with the licensor's R&D, both measured as a percent of sales or as a percent of the number of employees of both parties) is more important and more relevant than an absolute measure (such as the licensee's size).

Another reason, confirmed by the empirical results, is that there is a relationship between the royalty rate (as a measure of compensation) and the type of license agreement, on the one hand, and the number of restrictions in the license agreement, on the other. If the license does not compensate the licensor for the licensed technology in the form of a royalty, it has to do so in the form of more restrictions in the agreement. The licensed technology and the technical package have a price tag, regardless of the

TABLE 7.25 Summary of Empirical Results: Statistical Testing of Hypotheses (Licencees' Characteristics)

Licensees' Characteristics	Technology Life Cycle (Stage)		Type of Licensed Technology		Technical Uncertainty (degree)		Marketing Uncertainty (degree)		Royalty Rate (% of sales)		License Restrictions (number)	
	Earlier	Later	Related	Unrelated	Low	High	Low	High	Less Than 3%	More Than 3%	One or Less	Two or More
Small & medium	10 H1	27	27 H2	10	24	13	25	12	20	17	18	17
Large	9	5	5	9	6	8	6	8	7	7	8	6
With Core skills	13 H3	10	11	12	8 H4	15	6 H5	17	18	5	15	8
Without core skills	8	20	21	7	18	9	20	7	12	16	12	16
Dominant	10	8	7	11	4	14	6	12	15 H6a	3	13 H6b	4
Nondominant	9	24	25	8	18	15	17	16	15	17	13	21

Note: Entries represent number of firms in each cell.
Source: Based on original material compiled by the author.

142

TABLE 7.26 Summary of Empirical Results: Statistical Testing of Hypotheses (License Agreement Type)

License Agreement Type	Cancellation of License by Licensee due to		Licensees' R&D Capabilities		Production Difficulty		Number of Restrictions	
	Patent Life/ Disagreement	Licensees' Competence	Decreased/ Unchanged	Increased	Decreased	Increased/ Unchanged	One	Two or More
Continuous	5	14	2	29	27	4	6	25
		H7a		H7b		H7c		H8
One-time	11	3	14	6	7	13	14	6

Note: Entries represent number of firms in each cell.
Source: Based on original material compiled by the author.

143

licensee's size, under normal and arm's-length arrangements.

The compensation for the licensed technology may take various forms, of which the royalty as a percent of net sales of the licensed technology is just one. Others include a lump-sum payment and cross-licensing arrangements, which might have been the case in the above inconsistencies. The licensees also may compensate the licensors through the number of restrictions in the licensing agreement. The restrictions may include geographical limitations, field of use, and procurement arrangements (tying clauses).

Still another reason is related to the royalty and its dependence on the nature of the industry and the type technology involved. The royalty rate is more related to the nature and amount of the licensed technology and the nature of the industry than to the size of the licensing participants. The size of the licensee might be a factor in the licensor's choice of licensee (see Lodge & Shipley and Masstron cases).

There seems to be an inconsistency between the indirect implications of the research hypotheses (ex-ante) and the empirical results (ex-post) when the licensee's size and the number of restrictions in the license agreement are compared. This inconsistency relates to small and medium-sized licensees and the number of restrictions. The empirical results related to large firms are consistent with the expectations.

One reason is that the number of restrictions in the license agreement is more a function of the type of license agreement (continuous vs. one-time) than of the licensee's size. Also, the number of restrictions is more directly related to the nature of the industry and the type of licensed technology, as well as the amount of services (know-how) provided by the licensor to the licensee, regardless of the licensee's size. Hypotheses 6b and 8 support this argument, and there is no inconsistency between the predictions of the research hypotheses and the empirical results.

LODGE & SHIPLEY CORPORATION

Lodge & Shipley was established in 1890. Today, it is a medium-sized manufacturing firm that employs about 250 and has annual sales of approximately $20 million. The principal products of the company are (1) machine tools, (2) packaging machinery, and (3) metal end products.

The products in the machine tools segment are standard lathes and numerically controlled lathes. The primary products of the packaging machinery segment are case packers and uncasers for bottles. The primary products of the metal end products segment are components.

The principal users of the company's products are the defense, atomic energy, automobile, farm equipment, machine tool, aircraft, oil service, and brewing and soft drink industries. Therefore, the company's products play a role of strategic importance in U.S. industries.

Nineteen eighty-four was the third consecutive year of very depressed conditions in a large segment of the machine tool and machinery industries. Competition from imports into the U.S. market became even more intense, particularly as a result of the unexpected rise in the value of the dollar.

It now seems apparent that the U.S. government has no intention of limiting machine tool imports, and thereby preserving minimum capacity for machine tool manufacturing capability in this country. Accordingly, the company is making increased efforts to survive in this new environment, which can only be assumed to be a permanent way of life.*

Because of increased international competition and foreign imports, the machine tool industry suffers far more than any other basic industry. In the critical field of machine tools, the Japanese account for an astounding two-thirds of the total U.S. market, and so far as is known, there is no bona fide effort on the part of U.S. authorities to limit this volume.**

In order to survive, the company initiated a licensing agreement with Olivetti of Italy to import their line of small lathes. According to the company's 1984 annual report, its display at the 1984 International Machine Tool Show consisted soley of Olivetti products. As of 1984, the company had two licensing agreements, one from Italy and one from West Germany. Without such arrangements, it would not have survived.

Other U.S. firms were interested in a license from Olivetti but, according to Lodge & Shipley's president, the determining factor for Olivetti was the relative size of Lodge & Shipley. The licensor wanted to license its technology to a U.S. firm relatively smaller than itself that had an established line of products and a technical reputation.

The licensing arrangements gave Lodge & Shipley new and competitive technology to keep it afloat. As of early 1985, the company was negotiating with a company in Brazil to sublicense the technology it had acquired through licensing a few years earlier.

*Lodge & Shipley, Annual Report, Cincinnati, Ohio.
**Ibid.

8

Summary and Conclusions

SUMMARY AND CONCLUSIONS

Reverse licensing was defined as the international transfer of technology into the United States. This study focused on licensing of technology from the U.S. licensees' standpoint. Its objectives were to investigate the characteristics of U.S. licensees, their motivations for acquiring foreign technology, the extent of technology licensing, and the types of licensing agreements, and to look into the viability of reverse licensing as an alternative growth strategy.

The book began by focusing on a problem facing two groups of firms: the first is tens of thousands of small-to-medium-sized U.S. manufacturing firms, with one or a few products and with little or no funds spent on R&D. Without R&D and new and competitive products, they go bankrupt once their existing products reach the end of their life cycle. The importance of these firms in the states' and the nation's economy, particularly their job- and revenue-creating potentials, were documented.

The second group consists of a fairly large number of small and medium-sized foreign firms that have the technology (product) needed in the United States. It was argued that most of these firms are very anxious to enter the U.S. marketplace, as is evidenced by the number of U.S. patents granted to foreign nationals. Of various options available to them, licensing of their technology to U.S. firms was found to be the preferred alternative.

Consequently, there was an apparent gap between these two groups. A vehicle is needed for bridging the gap between the small and medium foreign firms with a poten-

146

tially good supply of technology and the small and medium-sized U.S. manufacturing firms that have a great demand for the technology. To overcome this problem, and to find the vehicle, the viability of reverse licensing as the missing mechanism was evaluated.

At the outset, the importance of licensing in international transactions, with the focus on the United States, was emphasized. Total U.S. licensing fees and royalties were more than $8 billion in 1984. Also, the U.S. income from royalties and licensing fees was almost 60 percent of the income from FDI.[1] Of course, this does not mean that licensing is 60 percent as important as FDI. This percentage is extremely important because licensing of technology has traditionally been considered a residual alternative to MNCs.

The postwar dominant role of the United States in international business and the international transfer of technology began to deteriorate in the late 1960s. Various factors were found to be responsible.

First, a decline in the number of R&D scientists and engineers in the United States; it had 66 percent of all R&D scientists and engineers in 1969, and ten years later its share had declined to 57 percent.[2] Also. R&D spending as a percent of GNP by other industrialized nations (for instance, West Germany) surpassed that of the United States.

Second, the industrial structure and productivity growth of the industrialized nations changed. An international comparison of R&D-intensive versus non-R&D-intensive manufactured products showed that the United States had a $179 million negative balance in 1960. This negative balance was almost $22.5 billion in 1980. The productivity growth in manufacturing industries deteriorated during 1960–82. While the compounded productivity growth for Japan was 480 percent, for France 207 percent, and for West Germany 187 percent, it was only 72.6 percent for the United States during that period.

Third, during 1973–83, the patents granted (as indicators of the degree of inventiveness) increased by 116 percent for western Europe combined and by 197 percent for Japan—and for the United States declined by 30 percent. Also, during 1970–80 foreign patents granted to U.S. nationals declined by 36 percent, while U.S. patents granted to foreign nationals increased by 42 percent.

Fourth, the ratio of royalties and fees (unaffiliated/affiliated receipts) was about 25 percent during 1975–83 and remained almost constant. That ratio for U.S. payments increased from 64 percent in 1973 to 165 percent in 1983. This indicates that U.S. corporations were buying more technology through licensing (from unaffiliated foreign sources).

Finally, U.S. corporations did not limit themselves to U.S. allies as foreign sources. Since the mid-1960s they have obtained needed technology from the Soviet Union and other Easter bloc countries as well. [3]

After showing the international position of the United States in technology licensing, R&D expenditures, patents, and productivity, it was argued that a contradiction exists between significant growth in foreign patent activities, on the one hand, and royalties and fees as indicators of international technology licensing, on the other. The conclusion was that perhaps U.S. firms are not utilizing reverse licensing to the extent that they should.

In Chapter 3, the focus was on international technology licensing. In order to understand the transfer of technology and to overcome semantics, technology was defined as a perishable resource comprising knowledge, skills, and other parts of the production process. While science organizes and explains data and observations by means of theoretical relationships, technology translates them into practical use. The transfer of technology may take place at the science, technology, or production level. There is no licensing of technology at the science level because there is nothing concrete to license.

At the next level—technology—licensing can be used for the transfer process. At this stage the technology is not commercially proven, and the licensee must have technical competence to understand, develop, and adopt it. The last stage is the production level. Even at this stage the licensee must have some engineering competence in order to adopt the technology. The transfer of technology was found to be either vertical (within a firm) or horizontal (between firms). The focus of this study was on horizontal transfers, with an emphasis on the licensee as the recipient of the technology.

The first section of Chapter 3 concluded by emphasizing the factors important for an effective technology transfer: (1) absorptive capabilities of the licensee, (2) the type of technology transferred, and (3) effective communication between the licensor and the licensee.

The focus was on the internationalization of technology and various alternatives open to the proprietor of technology for servicing the global markets. Exporting, licensing, joint-venture, and FDI as international market-entry strategies were introduced. This set the stage for focusing on technology licensing. It was argued that, traditionally, licensing was used as a residual alternative by most MNCs.

The licensors' motivations for licensing their technology were (1) to extend the technology's life, (2) to earn extra revenue not otherwise possible, (3) to enter a foreign market, (4) to establish and/or test the market for future production, and (5) to take advantage of cross-licensing arrangements. The main disadvantages of licensing to the licensor were the loss of control over the technology and the creation of a competitor.

The licensees' motivations for entering licensing arrangements were (1) to acquire the needed technology and avoid the risk of R&D expenditures, (2) to supplement their own existing R&D, (3) to acquire the right to operate, (4) to diversify and expand to related or unrelated operations, and (5) to cash in on the name and product of the licensor. The major disadvantages to the licensee were dependence on the licensor and the "NIH" syndrome.

The licensing issues, discussed in detail, were found to be (1) the negotiation process, (2) the compensation arrangements, (3) the legal aspects of licensing, (4) the licensee-licensor relationship, (5) the license agreement, and (6) the licensing impacts. In this book, the emphasis was on the compensation arrangement, the types of license agreements, the impacts of licensing, and the licensees' characteristics. The research hypotheses dealt with most of these issues.

The licensees' motivation for technology licensing and the cases for and against licenses were discussed. The cases in favor of taking a license were (1) cost of own R&D, (2) probability of failure, (3) timing involved, and (4) the patent laws.[4]

Next, the focus was on reverse licensing and its importance compared with reverse investment (FDI). In comparing reverse licensing with reverse investment, it was argued that there are thousands of small-to-medium-sized firms overseas that are technologically rich and very anxious to enter the U.S. market. But they do not have the resources (such as finances or marketing) and there is no mechanism facilitating their search for global reach. Licensing of their technology to a U.S. firm would be the best possible option open to these firms. Only a few hundred large foreign MNCs can afford the costs and the risk of investing in the United States. Since foreign MNCs are few in number, each state in the United States tries hard and makes various concessions to entice these MNCs to invest in their states.

At the same time, every year thousands of small-to-medium-sized U.S. firms are forced into bankruptcy because they have one or a few products and spend little or no money on R&D. They fail once their product(s) reach the end of the PLC. Because of its employment effect, the absence of tax concessions and political reprecussions, and costs, reverse licensing not only would do what reverse investment does but also would give these U.S. firms new products and an extension on their lives.

A review of the literature showed that almost all the research studies to date have focused on licensing of technology from the licensor's point of view. The major emphasis has been on the pricing of technology, the profitability of licensing, the policy implications of technology licensing, and the viability of licensing as a growth-market entry strategy. Although most researchers have looked at licensing of technology as a residual alternative, a few have argued that this is not necessarily the case. Their argument sets the stage for a more general theorem in international business that incorporates international trade, FDI, and licensing.[5] While licensing of technology is "found money" to some, it is the dominant, if not the only, viable international strategy to others.[6]

Many scholars have focused on the speed of technology transfer within a firm (vertical) and between firms (horizontal). The consensus is that the transfer is faster and more effective vertically.[7] While some have emphasized the importance of internationalization of technology, which gives preference to FDI over licensing,[8] others have stressed the importance of the international marketing of technology.[9] A large number of scholars and practitioners have focused on ways of arriving at a licensing rate, a licensing base, and royalty payments.[10] Some have emphasized the dependence issue and have come to a general conclusion that the foreign licensees were dependent on their U.S. licensors.[11]

Finally, a fairly large number of scholars and institutions have focused on East-West trade and technology transfers, and are generally divided into two groups. The first group has concentrated on the technology transfer from West to East, and national security and defense issues.[12] The second group has focused on the reverse transfer of technology, and its business and military windfalls.[13]

In Chapter 5, earlier discussions were conceptualized and the specific focus was on reverse licensing. It was demonstrated that in developing strategies for future technological needs, a firm has two options: (1) developing new technology independently and internally, or (2) acquiring the needed technology through licensing.

Depending on the characteristics of the firm and the nature of the industry, the firm might have various alternatives in its strategy formulation. If the firm is technically competent, it might develop the needed technology by using its internal resources, or it might be more economical to take a license. A license might be on a one-time or a continuous basis, each having its own advantages and disadvantages.

If, however, the firm is technically incompetent, the alternatives would be different. The firm might decide to build its own core skills first and then develop the needed technology. This is a very costly and uncertain strategy because of the risks and costs involved, as well as because of the probability of failure. In addition, most small-to-medium-sized firms do not have the resources and financial capabilities to withstand the international competition and to go through the long process.

Alternatively, the firm without core skills might choose to go the licensing route. Taking a license on a one-time basis would not be enough in most cases, because the firm does not have the technical competence to understand the technology, not to mention to adopt it.[14] Or the firm might decide to take a license on a continuous basis. Taking a license is perhaps the best strategy, provided the firm, as part of its strategic planning, gradually builds its own in-house core skills. The LCM dealt specifically with this group of firms.

The NPV technique for evaluating various options open to the licensees was introduced, and emphasized that all the relevant incremental cash flows on an after-tax basis must be used. Then the alternative with the highest positive NPV should be selected. Of particular interest in the analysis was the using of the appropriate discount rates or the adjusted cash flow (certainly equivalent), because not all options have identical return/risk characteristics (see Chapter 5).

Finally in Chapter 5, eight hypotheses were proposed as part of the research model. The first six dealt with licensees' characteristics (size, technical competence, and so on), the PLC, and the licensed technology characteristics. The last two focused on the type of license agreement (one-time, continuous), the LCM, and the types of restrictions in the license agreements.

In Chapter 6, the focus was on how the sample was selected and how the research instrument was designed. Alto, the statistical design and the logic behind it were discussed. Chi-square (χ^2), gamma, and the Spearman-Brown correlation coefficient (r^2) were introduced as the test statistics. χ^2 was used to test the null hypotheses for independence between research variables. To adjust for discrete data, the continuity-adjusted χ^2 was used. Gamma was also used to show the degree of association between the variables.

In Chapter 7, the hypotheses were empirically tested. After a pilot study of 30 U.S. licensees and a very strong reliability coefficient ($r^2 = .94$) using the Spearman-Brown formula, the questionnaire was mailed to 118 Ohio firms involved in reverse licensing. After the second mailing and the follow-up telephone calls, 51 questionnaires were considered complete and usable (a 43 percent response rate). Interviews with 10 licensees' executives followed, to shed more light on the statistical analyses.

Prior to the discussion of the empirical results, the characteristics of the licensees and the types of license agreements germane to this research will be reviewed.

LICENSEES' CHARACTERISTICS

Licensees' Size and the PLC

According to Vernon, the internationalization of business goes through the firm's PLC.[15] In the introduction stage, the firm produces for the domestic market; it is not until the second stage (growth) that the firm exports to foreign markets. In the later stages, the domestic market may be served through imports. (The PLC was discussed in detail in Chapter 3.) Here the focus is on two things.

First, the licensees are categorized, in terms of their annual sales or number of employees, into small, medium, and large. The argument is that the licensee's size does matter in international licensing. Also, small-to-medium-sized licensees are generally more likely to take a license once their existing product(s) reach(es) the declining stage of the PLC. If they want to stay competitive—if not afloat—they have either to develop new technology or to acquire it through licensing. Various options open to these firms have already been explained.

Second, these firms tend to take a license to manufacture products similar to their existing product line. This is because their resources (production, financial, marketing) and expertise are devoted to their existing line of business. As a result, the costs will be lower and the adaptation process easier than for nonrelated technology.

Licensees' Technical Competence and the PLC

The licensees' technical competence was explained in Chapters 6 and 7. Here, the argument is that there is a direct relationship between the PLC and licensees' competence. This implies that when technology is in a certain stage of the PLC, certain types of transfers can (cannot) take place. For example, when the licensee is technically competent, technology transfers take place at both the technology and the production levels (see Chapter 3). But licensees without core skills are limited to the production level, where technology is standardized.[16]

The License Agreement Types

The agreement types were explained in detail in Chapter 6. Briefly, there are two types: continuous and one-time. When the agreement is on a continuous basis, the licensor must be compensated either through royalties or through restrictions in the agreements. When the agreement is for one-time, the costs to the licensee will be lower, but it does not have access to technology advancements made by the licensor.[17]

THE RESEARCH RESULTS

The research findings are classified into two categories, general and specific, and are presented in the following sections:

General Findings

- Eighty-four percent of Ohio licensees had some form of international exposure prior to the licensing agreement, ranging from exporting to full overseas manufacturing, sales, and service facilities.

- Fifty percent of the time, Ohio licensees located the needed technology through direct marketing effort by the licensee and through personal contacts.

- Foreign governments were instrumental in the license agreements twice as often as U.S. governmental bodies.

- West Germany, Japan, the United Kingdom, the Netherlands, and Canada dominated the list of home countries of licensors.

- Nonelectrical manufacturing (SIC 35), chemicals (SIC 28), fabricated metal (SIC 34), and stone, clay, and glass (SIC 32) accounted for more than 80 percent of the licensed technology.

- Licensees' motivations for technology licensing were supplementing their own R&D (38 percent), diversification (36 percent), avoiding R&D risks (32 percent), and patent rights (26 percent).

- Eighty percent of the licensees' products were in the mature or declining stage of the PLC prior to licensing arrangements.

- Seventy-three percent of small and medium-sized licensees acquired similar (related) technology in the later stage of PLC, compared with 64 percent of larger licensees.

- Sixty-one percent of the licensed technology was either the mature or the standardized stage of the PLC in the licensor's market; 39 percent of the technology was at an earlier stage.

- Licensees with core skills acquired the technology in its earlier stages 56.5 percent of the time; 71 percent of those without core skills acquired technology in later stages.

- Sixty-five percent of licensees with core skills acquired technology where technical uncertainties were relatively high; 66 percent of those without core skills acquired technology with lower degrees of uncertainties.

- The percentages for marketing uncertainties were 74 percent and 74 percent, respectively for each group.

- In compensating the licensor for the technology, percent of net sales was the method most widely used by the Ohio licensees.

- A size comparison of the Ohio licensees with their foreign licensors showed that 68 percent were smaller, 10 percent were of equal size, and 22 percent were larger.

Specific Findings

The statistical testing of the research hypotheses resulted in the following findings:

- Small-to-medium-sized manufacturing firms tend to look for and acquire new technology (product or process) once their existing technology is at the declining stage of the technology life cycle. They usually lack competent in-house R&D and core-skill personnel.

- They search for and acquire more related and similar technology than unrelated technology. Their motive for the acquisition of technology is directly related to their existence; and because of their relatively limited resources, they have to acquire similar technology. The transfer process and the adaptation of technology are much easier and least costly to them.

- Firms with technical competence acquire more licenses on newer technology than do those without. Their technical competences enables them to understand the technology at the earlier stages of the PLC. Such is not the case for firms without qualified scientists and engineers.

- Technically competent firms acquire licenses to manufacture where the technical uncertainties are relatively high. This is directly related to the PLC stages. The relationship between the PLC and technical uncertainty was explained in Chapters 3 and 7.[18]

- Firms with core skills acquire licenses to manufacture where marketing uncertainties are higher than do those without. This was explained in detail in Chapter 7, and an analogy was made between the adoption process in marketing and marketing uncertainties.[19]

- There is an inverse relationship between the licensee's dominant characteristics (compared with its licensor) and the licensing fees. The greater the dominant characteristics (such as size) of the licensee, the lower the royalty rate and the lower the number of restrictions imposed by the licensor (see hypotheses 6 and 8 in Chapter 7).

- Licensees with continuous license agreements are more likely to acquire R&D competence than are those with one-time agreements, provided they build their own in-house R&D throughout the agreement. This implies that the licensees which go through the LCM have a better chance of achieving technical competence, mastering the technology, and reducing their dependence on the licensors.

- There is a direct relationship between the type of license agreement and the number of restrictions in the agreement. The lower the amount of technology (such as patent rights and technical know-how) transferred, the lower the number of restrictions. Therefore, when the agreement is on a continuous basis, the amount of technology transferred (such as the licensee's access to the licensor's R&D results) will be higher, as will the number of restrictions imposed on the licensee (such as geographical, procurement).

THE RESEARCH IMPLICATIONS

The implications of this research study will be discussed from three different angles: (1) the U.S. manufacturing firms in general and small and medium-sized firms in particular, (2) the foreign firms (as licensors), and (3) the governmental bodies.

U.S. Manufacturing Firms

This study began with a single question: Is reverse licensing a viable option for U.S. (Ohio) manufacturing firms? Throughout the study, it was demonstrated that under certain conditions, reverse licensing was perhaps the best alternative available to U.S. manufacturing firms that need new and competitive technology to survive and prosper (see Chapters 5 and 7).

It was also argued that most of these firms (especially the small ones) go bankrupt once their existing technology reach(es) the end of the PLC. They have various options, and taking a license from a foreign source was the preferred option in most cases. This option is extremely important to the existence of many firms, especially small and medium-sized ones, as was evidenced throughout the study.

This possibility is perhaps the one least explored by U.S. firms. The analysis supports the proposition that reverse licensing must be explored more by U.S. manufacturing firms. Of particular importance in this regard are the astronomical cost of R&D and the comparative advantages that foreign firms have over their U.S. counterparts.

The costs of R&D are extremely important to small U.S. firms that do not have the financial resources to engage in R&D. Reverse licensing will allow these firms access to foreign R&D and to the compensations directly contingent on the success of the licensed technology and the U.S. licensees. The very successful corporations in the United States have been utilizing this alternative for decades (see Chapter 2). The research findings clearly support this strategy.

Of course, this is not a prescription for all firms regardless of their firm-specific and industry-specific characteristics. A firm with a low R&D competence in a very innovative industry cannot (and should not) use the licensing option on a continuous basis without building its own in-house R&D. A direct result of such a strategy would be technological dependence on the licensor, assuming the licensor would be willing to license its state-of-the-art technology.

But if the firm builds its own in-house R&D throughout the agreement (LCM), or if the firm is in an industry where technological changes are not that frequent, reverse licensing would be among the best (perhaps the very best) strategies.

There is a direct relationship between the amount of R&D spending, as the inputs, and the amount of inventions and innovations, as the outputs.[20] The statistics provided in Chapter 2 support this argument and are perhaps among the very significant factors contributing to the deterioration of the U.S. industrial base. In short, U.S. manufacturing corporations should not limit themselves to sources within the United States, and should explore reverse licensing as a viable option. Technology licensing might be a residual alternative to licensors but, based on the findings of this study, taking a license (as a licensee) is not a residual one.

Firms with core skills that take license on a continuous basis (in most cases doing it because of cost considerations) should realize that the alienation of their core skills (the NIH syndrome) should not be taken lightly. Even though the licensed technology might be an asset to the licensee, its own core skills are by no means liabilities.

Small and medium-sized firms are of particular interest in this study because of their importance in the economy, especially their job-creating capabilities. A *Business Week* (May 27, 1985) report predicted that 52.7 percent of new jobs will be created by firms with 100 or fewer employees and 29 percent by companies with 100 to 999 employees.

Foreign Firms

In Chapters 1 and 3, it was demonstrated that there are thousands of small and medium-sized firms overseas that are technologically rich and very anxious to enter the U.S. market, but lack the required resources to invest directly. It was argued that from among various options available to them, licensing of their technology to U.S. manufacturers was the most often preferred alternative. For many of these firms, licensing was the only way of exploiting their technology needed in the United States.

A direct implication of this book and research study for foreign firms having a fairly large supply of technology is that reverse technology transfer provides them with opportunities to exploit the U.S. market that would be impossible otherwise.

Reverse licensing will probably be the only viable mechanism for matching the foreign supply of technology with the U.S. demand for it. The advantages of reverse licensing to small and medium-sized firms will be much more than those to large firms, because small and medium-sized firms lack the required resources to exploit other options.

As a result of reverse licensing, foreign firms will have revenues not otherwise possible, and this "found money" will enable them to do more R&D and produce more inventions and/or innovations. The "found money" for many of these foreign firms is the key to their existence. In Chapter 2, it was shown that foreign inventors have increased their patenting activities drastically and in some cases have surpassed that of the United States.

One implication of these increased patenting activities in general and the U.S. patents granted to foreign inventors in particular (almost 50 percent of all U.S. patents have been granted to foreigners in recent years—see Chapter 2) is that foreigners actively seek to exploit the U.S. market. But the data on royalties and licensing fees indicate that U.S. firms have not been utilizing the foreign sources of technology to the extent that they should. Reverse licensing undoubtedly will bridge this gap.

Governments

In recent years, governments (especially state governments) have drastically increased their involvement in international trade and reverse investment. Across the United States, legislatures have been studying the ways and means of boosting U.S. exports (state exports) and reverse investment. To match the international challenge of the 1980s and 1990s, and to remedy the U.S. ills and poor performance in the international markets (for instance, a $148 billion trade deficit in 1985), governmental bodies have introduced and adopted new incentive programs.[21]

These programs are essentially of two types. The first is designed to boost U.S. exports, and includes incentive programs ranging from a seminar on international trade to the formation of export trading companies and state export financing facilities.

The second type of incentive program at the state level includes promotional offices at home and abroad. These offices have various forms but more or less the same goal: to entice foreigners to invest in the United States (explained in Chapter 3). Various states have been competing with each other in getting the non-U.S. MNCs (a few hundred total) to invest in their states. In some cases, state initiatives have prompted federal concerns, and in others, federal programs have created state responses.

Governmental bodies have good reasons for such developmental and promotional programs: these programs have positive impacts on the economy, save and increase jobs, lower unemployment, and perhaps increase tax revenues. In 1983 alone, because of a $14 billion decrease in the export of U.S. goods and services, 300,000 American jobs were lost. In the period 1980–83, 1.5 million jobs were lost.[22]

FDI (reverse investment) in the United States has produced millions of jobs. According to Department of Commerce data, as a result of FDI, 2,343,115 jobs were created throughout the nation in 1981, of which 97,018 were in the state of Ohio.

Reverse licensing could provide the same number of jobs and amounts of revenues as reverse investment, with perhaps more advantages and less political backlash (see Chapter 3). The empirical results (Chapter 7), particularly those of the researcher's interviews with licensees' executives, reinforced this argument (see Chapters 3 and 7).

Because of its advantages, various governmental bodies (state administrators, legislatures, the Small Business Administration, the Export-Import Bank, the U.S. Department of Commerce), should seriously consider reverse licensing as a viable option in their struggle for the creation of a global mentality in the United States. Instead of, or at least parallel to, the existing reverse investment programs, reverse licensing should be considered and promoted.

This study was to investigate reverse licensing as an alternative to the development of own in-house R&D, and the conditions under which U.S. licensees take manufacturing licenses from foreign sources. The licensees' characteristics, the type of licensed technology, and the types of license agreements were among its findings. In order for this study to be complete, it is appropriate to talk about the research limitations and related future research.

THE RESEARCH LIMITATIONS

The sample size of 51 for this study (a 43 percent response rate is considered relatively good) was relatively too small to allow for higher levels of resolution in the bivariate analysis for the test of the hypotheses. Because of such limitations, the author had to collapse columns and rows in x^2 and contingency tables so that the expected frequencies in each cell would be 5 or more. This allowed the statistical analyses and interpretation of the test results.

Because of trade secrets and privileged information, and the limited availability of public information as part of international licensing, it is almost impossible to do some types of research studies (such as time series, regression, and multivariate). For most of such studies, an accurate, reliable, and comprehensive data base is required (such as CRSP or COMPUSTAT). These limitations are, at least so far, part of the game. The researcher therefore has a limited number of options in undertaking research in international licensing. The research on this topic will be limited to the methodology employed in this study or case studies where a relatively small number of firms are evaluated on a case-by-case basis.

With increased international licensing in general, and reverse licensing in particular, more attention should be given to the topic and more data will be available. Also, more scholars and practitioners will be involved in international licensing scholarly activities and new research methodologies will be developed.

Finally, this study focused specifically on reverse licensing as an alternative to the development of the firm's own in-house R&D and omitted many related subjects and issues in international technology licensing. Many of these issues might have a material impact on the conclusion of this study and the recommended options.

One of these issues, not part of this research, is the legal issues and tying clauses in international licensing of technology. This might have changed some of the recommendations. Another issue is the tax treatment of international licensing of technology. Different tax treatment of licensing fees (royalty payments) might have a material impact on the choice of a firm in search of new technology. Also, this research focused on Ohio manufacturing licensees (the reason for the small sample size); and the research findings, though of general application, are limited to Ohio licensees.

The last limitation of this study is related to financial resources (costs) and time. Had it not been for budgetary limitations, more interviews with licensees' executives could have been arranged. The interviews, in addition to being interesting, were very informative and provided the researcher with ideas not predicted in the questionnaire.

SUGGESTIONS FOR FUTURE RESEARCH

There are research areas directly related to this book that could be considered for further research in international technology transfer in general and technology licensing in particular. The following is a list of related research topics for future consideration:

1. A directly related, or perhaps similar, study would be a duplication of this study in other states. The goal could be to see whether the findings are generally applicable for all U.S. manufacturing firms or whether they are limited to the Ohio licensees.

2. A directly complementary study would deal with the licensors of the Ohio licensees, investigating their characteristics and their motives for licensing their technology.

3. This study focused on Ohio licensees and their characteristics, and evaluated technology licensing (from that perspective) as an alternative to own in-house R&D development. Another study could compare technology licensing with other options, such as joint ventures or reverse investment. Such a study could investigate the conditions under which each of these alternatives would be a preferred strategy.

4. A fourth possibility would be industry-specific and would focus on one or a few industries. It should take the licensee's standpoint, and investigate their characteristics (for instance, electronics industry vs. chemicals) and their motives for taking licenses from foreign sources. This type of research could be done for any manufacturing industry throughout the United States or internationally.

5. A fifth possibility for future research would build on the existing research, particularly on the LCM. The goal should be to investigate the viability of the LCM as a route to the development of in-house R&D. In this way further investigation of LCM would shed light on its general applicability, and whether LCM is more applicable to certain industries or firms than to others.

Such a study could be of utmost importance to U.S. businesses (large and small).

6. Another study in international technology would be firm-specific with regard to international marketing of technology. The research would deal with such questions as why some firms (Westinghouse) license their technology and others (IBM) will not license at all.

7. Another study might focus on a firm's size (small or large) as the determinant of its choice of R&D and its technical competence. It would investigate the conditions under which each alternative would be preferred.

8. Another future study might focus specifically on licensing compensation arrangements and pricing from the licensee's point of view. It would investigate pricing methods, and as its central theme would search for an optimum pricing strategy (or model) from a licensee's standpoint.

9. Finally, a futures study could focus specifically on marketing uncertainties in international technology licensing (hypothesis 5). The questions to be answered or investigated might deal with the conditions under which a licensee receives marketing know-how from its licensor or why some licensees will not license if the licensor's trademark is to be used (under what conditions could this be an acceptable option or strategy?). The study could investigate the relationship between the licensees' motives and the types of license agreements, with particular emphasis on marketing. Related questions might deal with the reasons why some licensors license their technology only under their name, while others let the licensees use their own names and trademarks.

Notes

CHAPTER 1

1. The term "reverse licensing" was first used by Prof. Lee C. Nehrt in an unpublished report to the Port Authority of New York and New Jersey (1979).

2. *The State of Small Business: A Report of the President Transmitted to the Congress* (Washington, D.C.: Small Business Administration Fact Sheet, U.S. Government Printing Office, March 1984).

3. Ibid., p. 36. Jobs were lost more readily in branches and subsidiaries of multi-establishment enterprises that closed between 1980 and 1982. While large firms do not often close headquarters offices, the branch closure rate increased 300 percent between 1980 and 1982, compared with 1978–80.

4. Ibid, p. 40.

5. See "Defense Windfall: Technology Purchased from Soviets Starts to Yield Military Uses," *Wall Street Journal*, April 24, 1985; "Soviet Technology Yields Ideas That U.S. Firms Can Exploit," ibid., April 25, 1985.

6. See Alan M. Rugman et al., *International Business* (New York: McGraw-Hill, 1985).

7. See *The State of Small Business*, p. 38.

8. See, for example, R. Ajami and D. Ricks, "Motives of Non-U.S. Multi-national Corporations for FDI in the U.S.," *Journal of International Business Studies* (Fall 1981); J. Arpen, C. Flowers, and D. Ricks, "Direct Foreign Investment in the U.S.," ibid.; John Daniels et al., *International Business Environment and Operation* (Reading, MA: Addison-Wesley, 1982); S. H. Hymer, *The International Operations of National Firms* (Cambridge, MA: M.I.T. Press, 1976); Alan M. Rugman, "A New Theory of International Business: Internalization," *Columbia Journal of World Business*, Winter 1980; Alan Rugman, et al., *International Business* (New York: McGraw-Hill, 1985).

CHAPTER 2

1. National Science Foundation, National Science Board, NSB 83-1, *Science Indicators 1982* (Washington, D.C.: U.S. Government Printing Office, 1983), p. 4.

2. Ibid., p. 7.

3. Ibid., p. 22

4. Ibid., p. 23.

5. *Productivity in Manufacturing—A New Country Alignment?*, World Business Perspective no. 81 (Washington, D.C.: National Industrial Conference Board, 1984).

6. *Industrial Property Statistics* (Geneva: World Intellectual Property Organization, 1983).

7. National Science Foundation, National Science Board, NSB 83-1, *Science Indicators 1982* (Washington, D.C.: U.S. Government Printing Office, 1983), p. 8.

8. Ibid., p. 14.

9. Royalties and fees (a raw measure of international transactions) show the international licensing transactions and are generally published in the June issue of *Survey of Current Business,* published by the U.S. Department of Commerce.

10. "Defense Windfall: Technology Purchased from the Soviets Starts to Yield Military Uses," *Wall Street Journal,* April 24, 1985; "Soviet Technology Yields Ideas That U.S. Firms Can Exploit," ibid., April 25, 1985. Both give examples of how U.S. corporations can exploit and have exploited the technology acquired from the USSR.

11. The decline since 1971 has been 40 percent. See National Science Foundation, *Science Indicators 1982,* p. 13.

CHAPTER 3

1. Stefan Robock, *The International Technology Transfer Process* (Washington, D.C.: National Academy of Sciences, 1980), p. 2.

2. G. R. Hall and R. E. Johnson, "Transfers of United States Aerospace Technology to Japan," in Stefan Robock and K. Simmonds, eds., *International Business and Multinational Enterprise,* 3rd ed. (Homewood, IL: Richard D. Irwin, 1983), p. 416.

3. R. S. Rosenbloom and F. W. Wolek, *Technology and Information Transfers,* in J. P. Killing, "Manufacturing Under License in Canada" (Ph.D. diss., University of Western Ontario, 1975), p. 30.

4. See Robock, *International Technology Transfer Process,* p. 462.

5. See, for example, Alan M. Rugman, "A New Theory of International Business: Internalization," *Columbia Journal of World Business,* Winter 1980.

6. See Alan M. Rugman et al., *International Business* (New York: McGraw-Hill, 1985), p. 121.

7. Ibid., p. 122.

8. Ibid. See L. T. Wells, Jr., *The Product Life Cycle and International Trade* (Cambridge, MA: Harvard University Press, 1972).

9. See Rugman et al., *International Business,* pp. 126–30, for an analysis of the NPV method.

10. Ibid., p. 130.

11. R. Polli and V. Cook, "Validity of the Product Life Cycle," *Journal of Business,* October 1969, p. 385.

12. W. G. Friedman and G. Kalmanoff, *Joint International Business Ventures* (New York: Columbia University Press, 1961).

13. G. A. Bloxam, *Licensing Rights in Technology* (1972), in J. P. Killing, "Manufacturing Under License in Canada" (Ph.D. diss., University of Western Ontario, 1975), Chap. 3.

14. Perlitz (1980), p. 53.

15. A. F. Millman, "Technology Transfer in International Markets," *European Journal of Marketing* (U.K.) 17, no. 1 (1983):31.

CHAPTER 4

1. "Compensation and Costs in International Technology Licensing" (Ph.D. diss., University of Pennsylvania, 1980); "Technology Licensing Practice in U.S. Corporations—Corporate and Public Policy Implications," *Columbia Journal of World Business* 18, no. 3 (Fall 1983):80; "Technology Licensing Versus FDI—an Analysis of U.S. Department of Commerce," paper presented to National Science Foundation, June 1984.

2. Franklin R. Root and Farok Contractor, "Negotiating Compensation in International Licensing Agreements," *Sloan Management Review* 22, no. 2 (Winter 1981):23–32.

3. See J. Perlitz, "Compensation Arrangements in International Licensing" in *The Law and Business of Licensing in the 80's* (New York: Clark Boardman, 1984) p. 83.

4. Richard A. Brecher, "Optimal Policy in the Presence of Licensed Technology from Abroad," *Journal of Political Economy* 90, no. 5 (Oct. 1982):1070–78.

5. M. Finnegan and H. Mintz, "Determination of a Reasonable Royalty in Negotiating a Licensing Agreement . . . ," in *The Law and Business of Licensing in the 80's.*

6. See Baranson, J., and A. Harrington. "Industrial Transfers of Technology by U.S. Firms Under Licensing Arrangements: Policies, Practices, and Conditioning Factors." Developing World Industry and Technology, Mimeo-

graph 1977, p. 43.

7. See Richard E. Caves, Harold Crookell, and J. Peter Killing, "The Imperfect Market for Technology Licensees," *Oxford Bulletin of Economics & Statistics* 45, no. 3 (Aug. 1983), pp.249–67.

8. J. Behrman and W. Schmidt, "Royalty Provisions in Foreign Licensing Contracts," *Patent, Trademark, and Copyright Journal,* Fall 1959, pp. 440–54.

9. Contractor, "Technology Licensing Practices in U.S. Corporations."

10. Edwin Mansfield, Anthony Romeo, and Samuel Wagner, "Foreign Trade and U.S. Research and Development," *Review of Economics and Statistics* (Netherlands) 61, no. 1 (Feb. 1979):49–57.

11. David Teece, "Technology Transfer by Multinational Firms . . . ," *Economic Journal,* June 1977.

12. A. F. Millman, "Technology Transfer in International Markets," *European Journal of Marketing* (U.K.) 17, no. 1 (1983), pp. 26–47.

13. Ibid.

14. See R. Vernon and W. Davidson, "The Speed of Technology Transfer by U.S. MNCs to Overseas Subsidiaries and Independent Licensees" (1979), p. 63.

15. Ibid.

16. Edwin Mansfield, "Economic Impact on International Technology Transfer," *Research Management,* Jan. 1974, p. 16.

17. A. Benvignati, "International Technology Transfer Patterns in a Traditional Industry," *Journal of International Business Studies,* Winter 1983, p. 63.

18. Arthur Lake, "Transnational Activity and Market Entry in the Semiconductor Industry," National Bureau of Economic Research Working Paper no. 126 (New York: The Bureau, 1976).

19. J. Peter Killing, "Manufacturing Under License," *Business Quarterly* (Canada), Winter 1977, pp. 22–29.

20. J. Peter Killing, "Technology Acquisition: License Agreement of Joint Venture," *Columbia Journal of World Business* 24, no. 3 (Fall 1980), pp. 38–46.

21. D. Wills (1982) unpublished report presented to Canadian Ministry of Industry.

22. Harold Crookell, "The Transmission of Technology Across National Boundaries," *Business Quarterly,* Autumn 1973, pp. 22–28.

23. G. Tesar, "Corporate Internationalization Strategy Through Licensing Arrangements in Industrial Marketing," paper presented at annual meeting of Academy of Marketing Science, Akron, OH, Mary 4–6, 1977.

24. R. T. Carstairs and L. S. Welch, "Licensing and Internationalization of Smaller Companies . . . ," *Journal of Small Business Management,* June 1982, pp. 33–44.

25. See David Ford and Chris Ryan, "Taking Technology to Market," *Harvard Business Review* 59, no. 21 (Mar./Apr. 1981), p. 117.

26. Ibid.

27. Caves, Crookell, and Killing, "The Imperfect Market for Technology Licenses."

28. William Finan, *The International Transfer of Semiconductor Technology Through U.S. Based Firms* (New York: National Bureau of Economic Research, 1975).

29. Cave, Crookell, and Killing, see p. 286.

30. U.S. Department of Commerce, International Trade Administration, *Foreign Investment and Licensing Checklist for U.S. Firms* (Washington, D.C.: U.S. Government Printing Office, 1983), pp. 8–9.

31. Neil Ruzic, "How to Tap NASA Developed Technology," *Research Management* 21, no. 6 (Nov. 1978), pp. 38–40.

32. George Stuart, "Technology Transfer—Patents and Licenses," *Productivity & Technology* (New Zealand) no. 4 (Aug. 1979), pp. 10–13.

33. See Malcolm R. Hill, "International Industrial Marketing into Eastern Europe," *European Journal of Marketing* (U.K.) 14, no. 3 (1980), pp. 139–64.

34. John W. Kiser III, "Tapping Eastern Bloc Technology," *Harvard Business Review* 60, no. 2 (Mar./Apr. 1982), pp. 85–92.

35. Ibid., p. 45.

36. "Why U.S. Business Taps Soviet Bloc Technology," *Business Week* (industrial ed.) 2636 (May 12, 1980):122H, 122J.

37. "Defense Windfall: Technology Purchased from Soviets Starts to Yield Military Uses," *Wall Street Journal,* Apr. 24, 1985; "Soviet Technology Yields Ideas That U.S. Firms Can Exploit," ibid., Apr. 25, 1985.

38. See Mark Joelson, "United States Law and the Proposed Code of Conduct on the Transfer of Technology," *Antitrust Bulletin* 23, no. 4 (Winter 1978), pp. 381–85.

CHAPTER 5

1. See R. Vernon, "International Investment and International Trade in the Product Life Cycle," in John Dunning, ed., *International Investment* (Harmondsworth: Penguin, 1972); S. Hirsch, "The U.S. Electronics Industry in International Trade," in L.T. Wells, ed., *The Product*

Life Cycle and International Trade (1976) for detailed analysis of various uncertainties.

2. See Vernon, "International Investment and International Trade. . . ."

3. Harold Crookell, "The Transmission of Technology Across National Boundaries," *Business Quarterly*, Autumn 1973, p. 22–78.

CHAPTER 7

1. William Dolle, President, Lodge & Shipley, Cincinnati, OH. Interviewed by the author.

2. R. Vernon, "International Investment and International Trade in the Product Life Cycle," in John Dunning, ed., *International Investment* (Harmondsworth: Penguin, 1972), p. 305.

3. J. Peter Killing, "Manufacturing Under License in Canada" (Ph.D. diss., University of Western Ontario, 1975), p. 60.

4. See Stefan Robock and K. Simmonds, eds., *International Business and Multinational Enterprise,* 3rd ed. (Homewood IL: Richard D. Irwin, 1983), pp. 421–22.

5. Ibid.

6. For a comprehensive analysis of pricing of technology licensing see Finnegan and Mintz, "Determination of a Reasonable Royalty in Negotiating a Licensing Agreement," in *The Law and Business of Licensing in the 1980's* (New York: Clark Boardman, 1981).

7. Robert Goldscheider et al., "The Art of Licensing—from the Consultant's Point of View," *Les Nouvelles* 6 (1971), p. 166.

8. H. Enlow, "Computer Licensing to Change," ibid. 9 (1974), p. 232.

9. R. Conte, "Aid to Pharmaceuticals," ibid. 11 (1976):19.

10. L. J. Eckstrom, *Licensing in Foreign and Domestic Operations* (New York: Clark Boardman, 1974).

11. R. Hashbarger, "Maximizing Profits as a Licensee," *Les Nouvelles* 6 (1971), p. 113.

12. M. Talbott, "General Subject: Licensing; the Automobile Industry," ibid. 7 (1972), p. 88.

13. A. Coogan, "Industry Patterns in Licensing, Paper Products, and Machinery," ibid., p. 17.

14. Godfrey Orleans, "Pricing Licensing of Technology," ibid. 16, no. 4 (1982), pp. 3D–29.

15. L. S. Welch, "The International Markets of Technology: An Interaction Perspective," *International Marketing Review,* Spring 1985, pp. 41–53.

16. Ibid.
17. Killing, "Manufacturing Under License in Canada," p. 34.
18. See R. T. Carstairs and L. S. Welch, "Licensing and Internationationalization of Smaller Companies," *Journal of Small Business Management,* June 1982, p. 33; Welch, "The International Marketing of Technology," p. 45.
19. See Farok Contractor, "Compensation and Costs in International Technology Licensing . . . ," pp. 46–47.
20. William Dolle, President, Lodge & Shipley, Cincinnati, OH. Interviewed by the author.
21. Carstairs and Welch, "Licensing and Internationalization of Smaller Companies . . . ," a survey of Australian firms, found that these costs constitute 29 percent of total licensing costs.
22. See Welch, "The International Marketing of Technology," p. 42.

CHAPTER 8

1. Farok Contractor, "Licensing Versus FDI in U.S. Corporate Strategy: An Analysis of U.S. Data," paper presented to Social Science Research Council, June 2–3, 1983, p. 15.
2. National Science Foundation, National Science Board, *Science Indicators 1982* (Washington, D.C.: U.S. Government Printing Office, 1984), p. 4.
3. "Defense Windfall: Technology Purchased from Soviets Starts to Yield Military Uses," *Wall Street Journal,* Apr. 24, 1985; "Soviet Technology Yields Ideas That U.S. Firms Can Exploit," ibid., Apr. 25, 1985.
4. See G. P. Bloxam, *Licensing Rights in Technology* (1972), Chap. 3.
5. Farok Contractor, "A Generalized Theorem for Joint-Venture and Licensing Negotiations," *Columbia Journal of World Business,* Winter 1984, pp. 44–70.
6. See Contractor, "Licensing Versus FDI in U.S. Corporate Strategy," p. 1.
7. See R. Vernon and Davidson, "The Speed of Technology Transfer by U.S. MNCs to Overseas Subsidiaries and Independent Licensees" (1979); Edwin Mansfield, "Economic Impact on International Technology Transfer," *Research Management,* Jan. 1974, p. 14.
8. See, for instance, Richard E. Caves, Harold Crookell, and J. Peter Killing, "The Imperfect Market for Technology Licenses," *Oxford Bulletin of Economics & Statistics* 45, no. 3 (Aug. 1983), pp. 249–67.

9. See, for instance, David Ford and Chris Ryan, "Taking Technology to Market," *Harvard Business Review* 59, no. 2 (Mar./Apr. 1981), pp. 117–26.

10. See, for example, Godfrey Orleasn, "Pricing Licensing of Technology," *Les Nouvelles* 16, no. 4 (1982), pp. 3D–29; M. Finnegan and H. Mintz, "Determinantion of a Reasonable Royalty in Negotiating a Licensing Agreement . . . ," in *The Law and Business of Licensing in the 80's* (New York: Clark Boardman, 1978).

11. See, for instance, Killing, "Manufacturing Under License in Canada"; Arthur Lake, "Transnational Activity and Market Entry in the Semiconductor Industry" (New York: National Bureau of Economic Research, 1976); Wills (1982).

12. See, for instance, Malcolm R. Hill, "International Industrial Marketing into Eastern Europe," *European Journal of Marketing* (U.K.) 14, no. 3 (1980), pp. 139–64.

13. See, for instance, John W. Kiser III, "Tapping Eastern Bloc Technology," *Harvard Business Review* 60, no. 2 (Mar./Apr. 1982), 85–92; "Defense Windfall"; "Soviet Technology Yields Ideas. . . ."

14. L. S. Welch, "The International Marketing of Technology . . . ," *International Marketing Review,* Spring 1985, p. 43.

15. See R. Vernon, "International Investment and International Trade in the Product Life Cycle," in John Dunning, ed., *International Investment* (Harmondsworth: Penguin, 1972); S. Hirsch, "The U.S. Electronics Industry in International Trade," in L. T. Wells, ed., *The Product Life Cycle and International Trade* (1976); Killing, "Manufacturing Under License in Canada."

16. Ibid.

17. See Welch, "The International Marketing of Technology," for an analysis of these costs. See also Vernon, "International Investment and International Trade in the Product Life Cycle" (1979).

18. See also Vernon, "International Investment and International Trade. . . ."

19. Stefan Robock and K. Simmonds, eds., *International Business and Multinational Enterprise,* 3rd ed. (Homewood, IL: Richard D. Irwin, 1983), p. 421.

20. See, for example, W. Leonard, "Research and Development in Industrial Growth," *Journal of Political Economy,* Mar./Apr. 1971, p. 232.

21. *Business America* (U.S. Department of Commerce), May 27, 1985, p. 12.

22. Ibid.

Bibliography

"Acquiring and Marketing Technology—Industrial Research Institute Position Statement on Licensing of Technology." *Research Management* 22, no. 3 (May 1979):32–33.

Ajami, R., and D. Ricks. "Motives of Non-U.S. Multinational Corporations for FDI in the U.S." *Journal of International Business Studies* (Fall 1981).

Aliber, R. Z. "A Theory of Direct Foreign Investment." In *The International Corporation*. Edited by C. P. Kindleberger. Cambridge, MA: M.I.T. Press, 1970.

Arnold, Tom. "Basic Considerations in Licensing." *Les Nouvelles* 15, no. 3 (1981). Reprinted in *The Law and Business of Licensing in the 80's*. New York: Clark Boardman, 1984, p. 2A–73.

Arpen, J., C. Flowers, and D. Ricks. "Direct Foreign Investment in the U.S." *Journal of International Business Studies* (1981).

Baranson, J., and A. Harrington. "Industrial Transfers of Technology by U.S. Firms Under Licensing Arrangements: Policies, Practices, and Conditioning Factors." Developing World Industry and Technology, Mimeographed 1977.

Behrman, J., and W. Schmidt. "Royalty Provisions in Foreign Licensing Contracts." *Patent, Trademark, and Copyright Journal*, Fall 1959, p. 84.

Benvignati, A. "International Technology Transfer Patterns in a Traditional Industry." *Journal of International Business Studies,* Winter 1983, p. 63.

Bloxam, G. A. *Licensing Rights in Technology*, Chap. 3 in J. P. Killing, "Manufacturing Under Lincense in Canada . . . ," (1972).

Brecher, Richard A. "Optimal Policy in the Presence of Licensed Technology from Abroad." *Journal of Political Economy* 90, no. 5 (Oct. 1982):1070–78.

Budak, P., and J. Susbauer. "International Expansion Through Licensing: Guidelines for the Small Firm." *Journal of Small Business Management*, January 1977, p. 17.

Business International. *Organizing for Maximum Income from Foreign Licensing Agreements*. Management Monograph no. 27. New York: Business International.

Carstairs, R. T., and L. S. Welch. "Licensing and Internationalization of Smaller Companies: Some Australian Evidence." *Journal of Small Business Management,* June 1982, pp. 33–44.

Caves, Richard E., Harold Crookell, and J. Peter Killing. "The Imperfect Market for Technology Licenses." *Oxford Bulletin of Economics & Statistics* 45, no. 3 (Aug. 1983):249–67.

Collier, T. P. "Do's and Don'ts of Foreign Licensing Arrangements." *Business Abroad,* Feb. 1971, p. 346–50.

Conte, R. "Aid to Pharmaceuticals." *Les Nouvelles* 11 (1976):19.

Contractor, Farok Jamshed. "A Generalized Theorem for Joint-Venture and Licensing." *Columbia Journal of World Business,* Winter 1984.

—————. "Technology Licensing Versus FDI—An Analysis of U.S. Department of Commerce." Paper presented to National Science Foundation, 1984.

—————. "Licensing Versus FDI in U.S. Corporate Strategy—An Analysis of U.S. Corporations." Paper presented to Social Science Research Council, June 2–3, 1983.

—————. "Technology Licensing Practices in U.S. Companies: Corporate and Public Policy Implications." *Columbia Journal of World Business* 18, no. 3 (Fall 1983):80–88.

Coogan, A. "Industry Patterns in Licensing, Paper Products, and Machinery." *Les Nouvelles* 7 (1972):77.

Crookell, Harold. "The Transmission of Technology Across National Boundaries." *Business Quarterly,* Autumn 1973, pp. 22–28.

Daniels, J., et al. *International Business: Environment and Organization.* Reading, MA: Addison-Wesley, 1982.

Davies, H. "Technology Transfers Through Commercial Transactions." *Journal of Industrial Economics,* vol. 26 no. 2, Dec. 1977.

"Defense Windfall: Technology Purchased from Soviets Starts to Yield Military Uses." *Wall Street Journal,* Apr. 24, 1985, p. 1.

Eckstrom, L. J. *Licensing in Foreign and Domestic Operations.* New York: Clark Boardman, 1974.

Enlow, H. "Computer Licensing to Change." *Les Nouvelles* 9 (1974):232.

Finan, William. *The International Transfer of Semi-conductor Technology Through U.S. Based Firms.* New York: National Bureau of Economic Research, 1975.

Finnegan, M., and H. Mintz. "Determination of a Reasonable Royalty in Negotiating a Licensing Agreement: Practical Pricing for Successful Technology Transfer."

In *The Law and Business of Licensing in the 80's.* New York: Clark Boardman, 1978.

Ford, David, and Chris Ryan. "Taking Technology to Market." *Harvard Business Review* 59, no. 2 (Mar./Apr. 1981):117–26.

Franklin, J. J. "Patent Statistics as Technology Indicators." M.S. thesis, Georgia Institute of Technology, 1983.

Friedman, W. G., and G. Kalmanoff. *Joint International Business Ventures.* New York: Columbia University Press, 1961.

"Global Reach—Industry Is Shopping Abroad for Good Ideas to Apply to Products." *Wall Street Journal,* Apr. 30, 1985, p. 1.

Goldscheider, Robert, et al. "The Art of Licensing—from the Consultant's Point of View," *Les Nouvelles* 6 (1971):166.

Hall, G. R., and R. E. Johnson. "Transfers of United States Aerospace Technology to Japan." In Stefan Robock and K. Simmonds, eds., *International Business and Multinational Enterprise.* 3rd ed. Homewood, IL: Richard D. Irwin, 1983.

Hashbarger, R. "Maximizing Profits as a Licensee." *Les Nouvelles* 6 (1971):113.

Hill, Malcolm R. "International Industrial Marketing into Eastern Europe." *European Journal of Marketing* (U.K.) 14, no. 3 (1980):139–64.

Hirsch, S. "The U.S. Electronics Industry in International Trade." In *The Product Life Cycle and International Trade.* Edited by L. T. Wells.

Hymer, S. H. *The International Operations of National Firms: A Study of Direct Foreign Investment.* Cambridge, MA: M.I.T. Press, 1976.

Industrial Property Statistics. Geneva: World Intellectual Property Organization, 1983.

Joelson, Mark R. "United States Law and the Proposed Code of Conduct on the Transfer of Technology." *Antitrust Bulletin* 23, no. 4 (Winter 1978):381–85.

Johnson, T., and J. E. Vahlne. "The Internationalization Process of the Firm—A Model of Knowledge Development and Increasing Foreign Market Commitments." *Journal of International Business Studies,* Spring/Summer 1977.

Killing, J. Peter. "Technology Acquisition: License Agreement or Joint Venture." *Columbia Journal of World Business* 15, no. 3 (Fall 1980):38–46.

——————. "Manufacturing Under License." *The Business Quarterly* (Canada), Winter 1977, pp. 22–29.

——————. "Manufacturing Under License in Canada."

Ph.D. diss., University of Western Ontario, 1975.

Kiser, John W. III. "Tapping Soviet Technology." In *Common Sense in U.S. Soviet Trade.* American Committee on East-West Trade, 1983.

──────. "Tapping Eastern Bloc Technology." *Harvard Business Review* 60, no. 2 (Mar./Apr. 1982):85–92.

Lake, Arthur. "Transnational Activity and Market Entry in the Semi-conductor Industry." National Bureau of Economic Research Working Paper no. 126. New York: NBER, 1976. Prepared for National Science Foundation.

Lee, Charles H. "How to Reach the Overseas Market by Licensing." *Harvard Business Review* 36 (Jan.–Feb. 1958):78–84.

Leonard, W. "R&D in Industrial Growth." *Journal of Political Economy,* Mar./Apr. 1971.

Licensing Executive Society. "Survey of International Technology Transfer from the United States: The Viewpoint of U.S. Technology Suppliers." Unpublished report.

Mansfield, Edwin. "Economic Impact on International Technology Transfer." *Research Management,* Jan. 1974, pp. 14–18.

Mansfield, Edwin, Anthony Romeo, and Samuel Wagner, "Foreign Trade and U.S. Research and Development." *Review of Economics & Statistics* (Netherlands) 61, no. 1 (Feb. 1979):49–57.

──────. *Technological Change and the Rate of Imitation in Industrial Research and Technical Innovation.* New York: W. W. Norton, 1968.

McFadden, Jack. "An International Licensing Agreement for Canadian Technology." *Foreign Investment Review* (Canada) 5, no. 2 (Spring 1982):12–14.

McLean, R. J. "Where Licensing Fits In." *Les Nouvelles* 16, no. 1 (1982), pp. 32–40.

Millman, A. F. "Technology Transfer in International Markets." *European Journal of Marketing* (U.K.) 17, no. 1 (1983):26–47.

Mirus, R. "A Note on Choice Between Licensing and Direct Foreign Investment." *Journal of International Business Studies,* Spring/Summer 1980, pp. 86–91.

National Industrial Conference Board. *Foreign Licensing.* New York: 1958.

National Science Foundation, National Science Board. *Science Indicators 1985—An Analysis of the State of U.S. Science, Engineering and Technology.* Washington, D.C.: U.S. Government Printing Office, 1986.

──────. *Science Indicators 1982—An Analysis of the State of U.S. Science Engineering and Technology.*

Washington, D.C.: U.S. Government Printing Office, 1984.

Nehrt, Lee C. "Reverse Licensing." Unpublished report to The Port Authority of New York and New Jersey, 1979.

Newfarmer, R. *The International Market Power of Transnational Corporations.* Geneva: UNCTAD, 1978.

Odagiri, H. "R&D Expenditures, Royalty Payments, and Sales Growth in Japanese Manufacturing Corporations." *Journal of Industrial Economics* 32, no. 1 (Sept. 1983):61–66.

Orleans, Godfrey. "Pricing Licensing of Technology." *Les Nouvelles* 16, no. 4 (1982):3D–29. Reprinted in *The Law and Business of Licensing in the 80's.* New York: Clark Boardman, 1984.

Perlitz, J. "Compensation Arrangements In International Licensing," in *The Law and Business of Licensing in the 80's.* New York: Clark Boardman, 1984, p. 53.

Polli, R., and V. Cook. "Validity of the Product Life Cycle." *Journal of Business,* Oct. 1969, p. 385.

Productivity in Manufacturing—A New Country Alignment? World Business Perspective no. 81. Washington, D.C.: National Industrial Conference Board, 1984.

"R&D: Where Spending Is Strong—and Getting Stronger." *Business Week* (special issue), Mar. 22, 1985.

Reddy, Elkins, and Rao. In *International Licensing: Some Strategy Considerations,* 1984.

Roberts, Ed B. "Is Licensing an Effective Alternative?" *Research Management,* Sept. 1982, p. 20.

———. "New Venture for Corporate Growth." *Harvard Business Review* 58, no. 4 (July/Aug. 1980):134–42.

Robock, Stefan. *The International Technology Transfer Process.* Washington, D.C.: National Academy of Sciences, 1980.

Robock, Stefan, and K. Simmonds, eds. *International Business and Multinational Enterprise.* 3rd ed. Homewood, IL: Richard D. Irwin, 1983.

Rodriquez, C. "Trade in Technical Knowledge and the National Advantage." *Journal of Political Economy,* Feb. 1975.

Rogers and Shoemaker. "Communication of Innovations." In *International Business and Multinational Enterprise.* Edited by Stefan Robock and K. Simmonds. Homewood, IL: Richard D. Irwin, 1983.

Ronstadt, R. *Research and Development Abroad by U.S. Multinationals.* New York: Praeger Publishers, 1977.

Root, Franklin R., and Farok Contractor. "Negotiating Compensation in International Licensing Agreements."

Sloan Management Review 22, no. 2 (Winter 1981):23–32.

Rosenblum, R. S., and F. W. Wolek. *Technology and Information Transfers.* Cambridge, MA: Ballinger, 1970.

Rugman, Alan M. "A New Theory of International Business: Internalization." *Columbia Journal of World Business,* Winter 1980.

Rugman, Alan M., et al. *International Business.* New York: McGraw-Hill, 1985.

Ruzic, Neil. "How to Tap NASA Developed Technology." *Research Management* 21, no. 6 (Nov. 1978):38–40.

"Soviet Technology Yields Ideas That U.S. Firms Can Exploit." *Wall Street Journal,* Apr. 25, 1985, p. 1.

The State of Small Business: A Report of the President— Transmitted to the Congress. Washington, D.C.: Small Business Administration/U.S. Government Printing Office, 1985.

The State of Small Business: A Report of the President— Transmitted to the Congress. Washington, D.C.: Small Business Administration/U.S. Government Printing Office, 1984.

Stuart, George. "Technology Transfer—Patents and Licenses." *Productivity & Technology* (New Zealand), no. 4 (Aug. 1979):10–13.

Talbott, M. "General Subject: Licensing; the Automobile Industry." *Les Nouvelles* 7 (1972):88.

Teece, David. "Technology Transfer by Multinational Firms: The Resource Cost of Transferring Technological Know-how." *Economic Journal,* June 1977.

Tesar, G. "Corporate Internationalization Strategy Through Licensing Arrangements in Industrial Marketing." Paper presented at the annual meeting of the Academy of Marketing Science, Akron, OH, May 4–6, 1977.

Tilton, John. *International Diffusion of Technology: The Case of Semiconductors.* Washington, D.C.: Brookings Institution, 1971.

Ting, Wenlee. "New Wave Multinationals Now Compete with Their Western Technology, Marketing Mentors." *Marketing News* 14, no. 8, sec. 1 (Oct. 17, 1980):12.

UNCTAD. *Major Issues Arising from the Transfer of Technology to Developing Countries.* TD/B/AC.11/10/Rev. 2. Geneva: United Nations, 1975.

Urban Institute. *Directory of Incentives for Business Investment and Development in the United States.* Washington, D.C.: Urban Institute Press, 1983.

U.S. Department of Commerce, International Trade Administration. *Foreign Investment and Licensing Checklist for U.S. Firms.* Washington, D.C.: U.S. Government

Printing Office, 1983.

U.S. Department of Labor, Bureau of Labor Statistics. *1986 U.S. Industrial Outlook.* Washington, D.C.: U.S. Government Printing Office, 1986.

"U.S. Making Overtures to Eastern European Nations." *Columbus Dispatch*, Dec. 9, 1984, p. 12A.

Vernon, R. "An Examination of International Product Life Cycle and Its Application to Marketing." *Columbia Journal of World Business*, Fall 1983, pp. 73–86.

——————. "International Investment and International Trade in the Product Life Cycle." In *International Investment.* Edited by John Dunning. Harmondsworth: Penguin, 1972.

Vernon, R., and W. Davidson. "The Speed of Technology Transfer by U.S. MNCs to Overseas Subsidiaries and Independent Licensees." 1979.

Welch, L. S. "The International Marketing of Technology: An Interaction Perspective." *International Marketing Review,* Spring 1985, pp. 41–53.

"Why U.S. Business Taps Soviet Bloc Technology." *Business Week* (industrial ed.) 2636 (May 12, 1980):122H, 122J.

Wiegner, Kathleen K. "Steel Turnabout." *Forbes* 126, no. 10 (Nov. 10, 1980):57–58.

Wells, Louis T., Jr. "A Product Life Cycle For International Trade?" *Journal of Marketing,* vol. 32, July 1968, pp. 1–6.

Index

About the Author

Manuchehr Shahrokhi is professor of finance at California State University, Fresno, California. Prior to joining C.S.U., he served on the faculty of finance at Franklin University and The Ohio State University (1983–1986). He taught finance and various international business management courses at Franklin University and The Ohio State University.

Prior to joining the academic world, Dr. Shahrokhi had an extensive business background and served as Chairman and CEO of Iran Rasht Electric Company, the largest manufacturer in the Middle East for three years, and seven years as senior overseas procurement analyst for National Iranian Oil Company in Tehran.

Dr. Shahrokhi has published in the areas of finance, international finance and international marketing management. As an academician, Dr. Shahrokhi was the recipient of the Outstanding Educator of the Year Award at Franklin University (1984). In addition, he is an active member of the Financial Management Association, American Finance Association, and the Academy of International Business.

Dr. Shahrokhi holds a BBA from Tehran Business School, MBA from The George Washington University, and Ph.D. from The Ohio State University.